Jacqueline Kennedy

A PORTRAIT IN COURAGE

Jacqueline Kennedy

A PORTRAIT IN COURAGE

By Hal Dareff

Illustrated by Tom Quinn

PARENTS' MAGAZINE PRESS

A Division of Parents' Magazine Enterprises, Inc.
New York

This book is for my wife, Gladys, a portrait in patience, and for our sons, Scott and Brooks.

1966
Second Printing

Contents

Childhood

CHAPTER ONE

The six-year-old girl jogged her horse into a trot. As he picked up speed she headed him for the wooden fence he was supposed to jump. Over and over again her mother had taught her to ride in straight when taking a jump. But this time she either forgot or ignored these instructions. Instead, she brought her mount in at an angle. At the last moment he shied away, skidding to a stop. His little rider went flying from the saddle and landed with a bump on the ground.

The spectators at the Southampton horse show still remember how she picked herself up instantly and tried to climb back into the saddle. In her haste she made the beginner's mistake of trying to get on from the wrong side of the horse. She really might have gotten hurt if one of the judges hadn't raced over quickly, grabbed her up in his arms, and carried her off to safety.

The crowd laughed. Then it broke into loud applause. Jacqueline Lee Bouvier was too angry to pay any attention. She stalked away, hopping mad, the sound of clapping still ringing in her ears. Being in the limelight was nothing new to little Jacqueline. Her small, jodhpur-clad figure was already a familiar sight at Long Island horse shows.

Jacqueline's mother, Mrs. John Vernou Bouvier III, was not surprised by her daughter's display of courage and temper that day. Whenever little Jackie acted brashly or had a tantrum, her mother had a ready explanation for her behavior. It was the "French" in her. This so-called Gallic strain in her ancestry belonged to her father's side of the family.

John Vernou Bouvier III came from a long line of Bouviers, many of whom still lived in France. The first Bouvier to come to America had been Jacqueline's great-

great-great-grandfather, André Eustache Bouvier. His family had lived in the town of Fontaine, near Grenoble. At the age of twenty-one young André had enlisted in the Grenoble Artillery Regiment and gone off to America to help the colonists fight King George and the British. He was even lucky enough to witness the British surrender at Yorktown in 1781, an experience he remembered all his life.

But after the war André had returned to France. Twenty-four other members of the Bouvier clan who had also fought under General Lafayette returned with him. It was André's son, Michel, who emigrated to America years later. He came to stay and settled down in the city of Philadelphia.

Once he had been a soldier in the armies of Napoleon. Now he became an importer of Italian marble and a manufacturer of veneer. He also married Louise Vernou, the daughter of a former French nobleman, and raised a family of ten children. Michel Bouvier worked hard and prospered. At his death he left a considerable sum of money for his wife and family. His friends in Philadelphia thought so much of him that they named a street after him—Bouvier Street—which is still there today.

One of Michel's ten children was the first John Vernou Bouvier, Jacqueline's great-grandfather. He also had the martial spirit in him and went off to fight in the Civil

War at the age of eighteen. He was badly wounded and spent the last part of the war in a Confederate prison camp. After the war he married a socially prominent girl named Caroline Ewing. John Bouvier had only one lung as a result of his war wound and it was thought by many that he wouldn't live very long. But he fooled everybody. When he died he had already passed his eighty-third birthday. He had also amassed a tidy fortune. His wife, a generous, warm-hearted woman, was known for her good works. It was she—as Caroline Bouvier—who founded one of the most famous charitable institutions in the country. It is called the New York Foundling Hospital. This place of mercy accepts all unwanted children and cares for them, no matter what their race, creed or color. Jacqueline must have thought a lot of this great-grandmother of hers. She and John F. Kennedy were to name their first child after her.

John and Caroline Bouvier had but one child. This was a son, John Vernou Bouvier, Jr., Jacqueline's grandfather. He was an old man in his seventies when his granddaughter got to know him. He was also quite a remarkable man in his own right. Only sixteen when he enrolled at Columbia University, he graduated with honors. His intelligence and scholarship won him membership in the very select Phi Beta Kappa Society. Later he became one of the most famous trial lawyers in the country. He was also a keen student of American history and a recognized expert on the United States Constitution.

One of his sons, John Vernou Bouvier III, was destined to become Jacqueline's father. Unlike the elder Bouvier, young Jack, as he was called by his friends, did not have a scholarly temperament. Instead, he liked sports and racing around in fast cars. He also stayed a bachelor for a long time. A successful stockbroker, he was already in his thirties when Jacqueline's mother caught his eye. He had known Janet Lee for years but had never given her even a second glance. She was the friend of his own teenage twin sisters, Maud and Michelle.

Both families—the Lees and the Bouviers—had summer homes in East Hampton. Handsome Jack Bouvier was what women call a "good catch." His dark good looks had won him the nickname of "The Sheik," because he reminded people of the movie idol of the day, Rudolph Valentino. Many girls had set their traps for him, but none snared him until pretty Janet Lee cast her net.

Only the summer before Jack Bouvier had looked upon Janet Lee almost without seeing her. But this summer—the one after her debut—was different. This summer he seemed to *see* her for the first time.

He was sixteen years older than she was, but that seemed to make no difference. He was thirty-six and she twenty when they married at St. Philomena's Church in East Hampton. The date was July 7, 1928. The noon reception at the Lee house was attended by five hundred guests. Meyer Davis and his orchestra, society's favorite music-makers, played gay tunes to which everyone danced. Then the happy couple sailed for Europe on the luxury liner, *Aquitania*. It was a fitting end to what had been the outstanding social event of the season.

Just a little more than a year later, on July 28, 1929, Jacqueline Lee Bouvier was born. The Bouvier's first child weighed exactly eight pounds at birth. She could not be called pretty as an infant, but as she grew older she also grew prettier. Her skin became rosy and clear. Her dark eyes flashed and snapped. Her black hair began to curl in ringlets.

People began to notice how much she looked like her father. The resemblance was striking—the same wide-set eyes, the same warm, sensual mouth, the same determined line of jaw. When Jack Bouvier looked at his daughter he saw almost a mirror image of himself. From the beginning there was a great closeness and warmth between father and daughter which was to grow with the years.

From the beginning, too, it was plain that Jack Bouvier's daughter had a style and a personality all her own. Jacqueline was a charming child. Her offbeat sense of humor was unusual for one so young. She was firmly independent and strong-willed. Her honesty—which was complete—could prove embarrassing. And she had a stubborn streak that was very trying at times. Her nurse, Bertha Newey, often had her hands full with her.

The world into which Jacqueline had been born was a special kind of world. It was a world of families with money and social position. What went on inside this world, where the favored few of society frolicked and played? Those who stood outside its high, forbidding walls were curious and wanted to know. So newspaper and magazine editors sent reporters and writers scurrying about to find out. A birth, a wedding, an engagement, a party—all these were news. Jacqueline found out very early in life that other people were interested in what she did.

Her first social press notice came at the age of two. It began: "Little Jackie Bouvier, daughter of Jack Bouvier and the former Janet Lee, will not make her bow to society for another sixteen years or more, but she was a charming hostess at her second birthday party given at the home of her parents, 'Rowdy Hall,' on Egypt Lane."

It went on to say that the twenty pint-sized guests had had a whopping good time riding ponies and playing games. They had also dug for prizes in a Jack Horner pie and polished off a huge birthday cake.

Jacqueline showed her mettle during the pony-riding session. Her mother had begun teaching her the fine points of horsemanship when she was one year old. At the age of two she was already a veteran with one year's training behind her. Everyone at the party was impressed with the easy, confident way she rode her pony.

Even her dog Hootchie barked with pride when he saw her. Hootchie, a black Scottish terrier, was Jacqueline's first pet. In her eyes he was the most beautiful dog in the world. A perky little rascal, he and Jacqueline cavorted across the lawns of East Hampton together.

Later that summer, Jacqueline "showed" Hootchie at an East Hampton dog show. A reporter covering the event described the unusual sight of Jacqueline and her dog: "Little two-year-old Jacqueline Bouvier toddled to the show platform and exhibited with great pride a wee Scotch terrier of about her own size."

The audience was delighted with Jacqueline, but the judges failed to award Hootchie a prize. Jacqueline was disappointed. She couldn't understand why her beloved Hootchie hadn't won a ribbon. Two other members of the family did win blue ribbons, though, for their entries—her Grandmother Bouvier and her Aunt Edith. That was some kind of consolation.

In the winters the Bouviers lived in an apartment in New York City. Summers were spent with friends and family in East Hampton. Jacqueline learned to divide the year into two parts—the winter part and the summer part. The New York apartment, a handsome duplex on fashionable Park Avenue, was a gift from Janet's father, banker James T. Lee. The Bouviers went to live in it when Jacqueline was one year old.

Jacqueline's favorite toys were stuffed animals. Her special favorite was a rag doll named Sammy. She dragged Sammy around with her everywhere, and at night he curled up beside her when she went to bed.

In the spring of 1933, early in March, the Bouviers added a new member to their family. Her name was Caroline Lee Bouvier. Jacqueline was three and a half years old when her baby sister was born. The new baby took over the room where Jacqueline used to take her afternoon naps. Now she had to nap in the big spare room which was later turned into a playroom for the two girls.

From the beginning everyone got into the habit of calling Jacqueline's sister by her middle name—Lee. This same sister grew up to marry a Polish nobleman and become the Princess Stanislas Radziwill. But when Lee was less than a year old and Jacqueline was a little over four, they were both part of a big adventure.

It happened in Central Park. Jacqueline and Lee had been taken there by the family nurse. After they were gone awhile, the phone rang in the Bouvier apartment. Jacqueline's mother answered. It was the police department! They had just picked up a little girl. They couldn't understand her name, but she had given them this telephone number to call. In no time at all Mrs. Bouvier was down at the station house. Sure enough, there was Jacqueline, busily talking to one of the officers. She looked up and saw her mother. "Hello, Mummy," she said calmly.

The officer who had found Jacqueline told Mrs. Bouvier how he had come across her wandering little girl. He had spotted Jacqueline walking alone on a path in Central Park. When she saw him, she walked up and said, "My nurse is lost." The officer chuckled and so did everyone else who was listening.

The poor nurse had indeed been "lost." When found, she was still looking for Jacqueline, walking up and down every path she could find calling her name. She had left baby Lee with another nurse while she went off on her fruitless search through the park. She was very relieved indeed to find that Jacqueline had not been kidnapped as she had feared.

Another favorite family story about Jacqueline as a child has to do with her attitude about telling the truth. There was an elevator operator in the apartment building named Ernest. Rarely, if ever, did Ernest crack a smile or even manage to look pleasant. His only outstanding feature was a shock of blond hair that stood up on top of his head as stiffly as a brush. One day Jacqueline and sister Lee got into the elevator. Little Lee looked up at Ernest and smiled sunnily. "You look pretty today," she said. Before Ernest could reply and thank her, Jacqueline had cut in angrily. "It isn't true!" she cried. "Ernest looks just like a rooster!"

As children, Jacqueline and Lee were very different. Lee was always polite and diplomatic. Jacqueline's manner was open and frank, almost to the point of bluntness. She moved and acted quickly, and was quick to anger, although she never held grudges. Lee, on the other hand, seemed to move slowly and cheerfully through life, and was always anxious to please. Opposites though they were, the two sisters were very fond of each other. Jacqueline sometimes lost her patience and temper with Lee, but she was also very protective toward her younger sister.

Jacqueline's formal schooling began at The Chapin School, a well-known private school in New York. Before that she had had a year of pre-school training at another private school for children of kindergarten age. The headmistress of The Chapin School was a very formidable lady named Miss Ethel Stringfellow. Most students were in dread of being naughty, for the punishment for misdeeds was a private session with the severe headmistress. Nobody knew exactly what it was that Miss Stringfellow did or said that struck such terror into the hearts of those who broke the law. Whatever it was, it seemed to do the trick. Not many of her correct little charges were willing to risk finding out.

Jacqueline was one of those dauntless few. For Jacqueline, as it soon became clear, was an out-and-out rebel. The other girls considered it a badge of shame to be sent to Miss Stringfellow. Not so Jacqueline, who seemed to look upon it as an honor. Her reputation as a mischief-maker grew and grew until, like Abou Ben Adhem, her name led all the rest in this department.

Janet Bouvier had good reason to suspect that Jacqueline was getting into occasional hot water at school. She wouldn't have been Jacqueline if she hadn't. But she had no idea that her daughter was engaged in a private daily war with the embattled headmistress. She learned about it by accident one day when one of Jacqueline's friends innocently spilled the beans.

True to her creed of absolute honesty, Jacqueline immediately admitted all when confronted by her mother.

"And what happens when you're sent to Miss Stringfellow?" she was asked.

"Well," said Jacqueline, "Miss Stringfellow says a lot of things—but I don't listen."

Miss Stringfellow, as it turned out, was not really the dragon the children thought her to be. She was a wise, knowing woman who had had many years of experience with children. Every child, she knew, could be reached somehow. All one had to do was find the right key.

The patient headmistress kept trying. Jacqueline kept turning a deaf ear to everything she said. It was a long struggle between two strong-willed females. But Miss Stringfellow would not give up. She knew Jacqueline as a bright, talented child, one who had, as she once said, "the most inquiring mind we've had in this school in thirty-five years." It would pay to tame this little rebel—but without breaking her spirit.

At last Miss Stringfellow found the way. One day Jacqueline, as usual, was sent to her office. Instead of speaking harshly to her, the headmistress took another tack. She knew that Jacqueline was absolutely mad about horses. So she asked her how she would feel if she owned the most wonderful racehorse there was and then discovered he couldn't be trained and wouldn't obey commands. It would be a terrible loss to everyone—to both the horse and his master—because all the greatness in the animal would never be realized. Then she told Jacqueline that she was very much like that horse who refused to be tamed. She was a thoroughbred, too, but it would all be wasted if she didn't settle down and learn to behave properly. And then no one would ever know that she had all the qualities of a champion because she had never allowed them to develop.

Jacqueline got the message. Overnight her attitude changed. She stopped being a steady visitor to Miss Stringfellow. Now she wanted to show Miss Stringfellow that she was one thoroughbred who wouldn't go wrong. She strove hard to impress the school head with her newfound sense of responsibility. Her work at school improved and she seemed a happier child overall. Jacqueline was always to look back upon this incident and to remember Miss Stringfellow fondly and gratefully as "the first great moral influence" in her young life.

Miss Stringfellow had indeed struck a responsive chord in Jacqueline when she brought up the subject of horses. Even at this tender age the little Bouvier girl was considered a fine rider. Trained by her mother, who was an outstanding horsewoman, Jacqueline quickly showed herself to be a chip off the old block. Janet was very proud of her five-year-old when they competed in the East Hampton Horse Show as a mother-daughter team and carried off third prize.

Janet Bouvier was known throughout the country for her skill as a rider and as an expert trainer of horses. She had ridden and competed in horse shows all over the East. Her feats and victories, over a period of many years, had made headlines in the newspapers and she had a batch of ribbons and trophies to prove it. She loved horses and had a special soft spot in her heart for those mounts who had shared her greatest victories with her. A trio of beautiful chestnuts with wonderful names—Stepaside, Clearanfast and Danseuse—and a bay mare named Arnoldean had been her favorites. Janet loved them so much that she kept them on as family pets after their competing days were over.

It was against this background of horses and horse shows that little Jacqueline grew up. From the time she could toddle she had known what it was like to sit in the saddle and feel the jogging motion of a horse under her. At first one of her parents held on to a lead line while she rode. But soon she was able to trot along all by herself. Her mother taught her how to sit easily in the saddle and how to maintain a posture of firm, moulded grace as she galloped. In no time at all she had picked up the fine points of handling horses. It was indeed a sight to behold this fearless little rider race along like the wind, come to a fence and clear it with a bold, flowing leap.

Her father liked horses, too, but he was more of a spectator than a rider. He and Jacqueline went to many horse shows together. Father and daughter were a familiar sight at these affairs and their pictures turned up often in the newspapers and magazines. One—taken when she was seven—had a caption underneath it which noted that "she has earned the distinction of being Long Island's youngest horse show fan—too young to rival her mother's feats, the promising young rider has been a spectator at every important contest for several seasons. Just mention the various horse shows, and little Jackie can reel off the winners in every class."

Jacqueline scored her first big riding triumph at the age of eight. She was pitted against lots of other good young riders at the Southampton Horse Show but managed to come out on top. It was a thrilling moment when she was presented with the winner's ribbon.

From then on Jacqueline began to be a serious contender for honors in any event she entered. Her greatest victories came when she was eleven years old. The exciting scene was Madison Square Garden in New York, where contestants had gathered from all over the United States. They were the winners of local shows in their areas who had won the right to compete in the national championships. A win here in one of the final events was the dream of every top young rider in the country. Jacqueline won *two*.

Here's how the New York *Times* reported it: "Jacqueline Bouvier, an eleven-year-old equestrienne from East Hampton, Long Island, scored a double victory in the horsemanship competition. Miss Bouvier achieved a rare distinction. The occasions are few when a young rider wins both contests in the same show."

Jacqueline's love for horses was never to waver or grow dim. Later, as a young teenager at school in Connecticut, she took along her very favorite horse to keep her company, the beautiful chestnut hunter, Danseuse. Jacqueline never scaled the riding heights that her mother did, but mainly because she did not choose to. Even as a child she was aware of other interests. For one thing, she discovered the wonderful worlds of books and art.

Books had come into her life at a very young age. One of her greatest pleasures before she could read was being read to at bedtime. The words and pictures stimulated and excited her imagination. A story could make you a princess being rescued by a prince, or a little girl like Dorothy going off to the magic land of Oz. You could share in the adventures of *Peter Rabbit* and *Winnie the Pooh*. Pictures were just as wonderful as words, for they turned dreams into reality. *There* was Dorothy, and *there* the Tin Man, and *there* the Cowardly Lion—just as large as life. And *Winnie the Pooh* wasn't just a made-up bear. He was as real and alive as the marvelous illustrations of E. H. Shephard had made him.

Being read to was fun, but Jacqueline wanted to read the words for herself. So she learned how, long before she went to school. Then she would sit by herself quietly and let the stories take her far beyond the walls of the Park Avenue apartment. She had a library of her own which grew larger each year. One of the most exciting times was at Christmas when Grandmother Bouvier, who knew what she wanted, always gave her books. But even her own books did not satisfy her curiosity. She roamed among her parents' bookshelves and read the books there. One afternoon, to her utter amazement, Janet Bouvier discovered that her daughter had been reading the stories of the Russian writer Anton Chekhov, which were way beyond her years. Not only that. She had understood the plot. To Janet's even greater astonishment, she sketched the outline of the story and asked her mother to explain certain words she hadn't understood.

It wasn't long before Jacqueline was writing her own stories and illustrating them with pictures which she drew. They showed a decided talent and Janet proudly began to save them.

She wrote her first poem at eight. Its title was *Christmas,* and it went:

> Christmas is coming
> Santa Claus is near
> Reindeer hooves will soon be drumming
> On the roof tops loud and clear
> The shops are filled with people
> Snow is coming down
> And everyone is merry
> In such a busy town.

Jacqueline kept writing poems. She liked to compose them in honor of special family occasions. When someone had a birthday or an anniversary, Jacqueline wrote a poem about it. She herself had been receiving birthday poems written about her by Grandfather Bouvier ever since she was one year old. Now Jacqueline had turned the tables. Grandfather Bouvier loved it and was one of her biggest fans. He was sure that Jacqueline had genuine literary ability and told her so. This was a great source of encouragement to his granddaughter.

Her sense of humor, which had always been wide and overflowing, also found its way into her writings. But though she often poked fun at friends and relatives in these compositions, her humor was gentle and never malicious. One of them interests us today. In it Jacqueline set down her predictions for the future about members of the family. There was also one about herself. She—she wrote—would end up as a circus queen. Rich and famous men would pursue her and beg for her hand, but she would spurn them all for "the man on the flying trapeze."

Many people who knew her in these early years, and later at college, thought she would take up a literary or artistic career. One of them, an English professor, said: "I always knew that Jacqueline would make a name for herself someday. But I really thought it would be by writing a book."

So did lots of other people, and there may have been a time when Jacqueline thought so herself.

Horseback riding and books, writing and drawing—these were Jacqueline's main interests during these formative years. But there was also another side to her—the tomboy side.

Her Bouvier cousins were mostly boys and Jacqueline found herself smack in the middle of them. There was only one way a girl could earn respect and acceptance by this wild brood and that was to do all the things they did. Every summer in East Hampton she had to prove all over again that she "belonged." This often led to dangerous deeds and escapades that sometimes had her hovering on the edge of disaster. But Jacqueline faced up bravely to every new challenge, just as she was to face up to every trying situation in her life. It was just like jumping a hurdle on a horse, she discovered. Some obstacles have to be met head-on to be conquered.

All girls have favorites among their cousins. Jacqueline had one, too, the son of one of her father's twin sisters. His name was Henry Clarkson Scott, but everyone called him "Scotty." Of all that bold band of junior daredevils and desperadoes, she liked him the best. Why? Because he was by far the baddest boy among them and always got into the most trouble. "Scotty" Scott was a fearsome climber of trees, and it was a red-letter day in Jacqueline's life when he invited her along for a tree climb with him.

There was another cousin whom she adored. This was Michel Bouvier, the son of her father's brother, Bud, who had died just before Jacqueline was born. Michel—nine years older than Jacqueline—had been her godfather at her christening. There was no real big brother in Jacqueline's life, but in her imagination she filled that empty place with Michel. The best thing about "Miche," as he was known, was that he didn't talk down to her. That was enough to make him "tops" to any young girl.

Miche also squired young ladies to parties and dances, which Jacqueline considered a very grown-up and glamorous activity. She was already getting her own first taste of ballroom dancing. Twice a week she went to Miss Hubbell's dancing classes at the swank Colony Club. Both boys and girls took part in these very formal, spit-and-polish occasions. Everyone had to dress in his very best—which included white gloves. When she donned a party frock and combed out her braids, Jacqueline made an almost magical transformation from a smudge-faced tomboy to a dazzlingly pretty girl.

Ballroom dancing was all right, but she *really* liked ballet. Only girls attended these classes. Jacqueline grew so fond of ballet that she read every book she could find on it. She also turned out to be a talented performer. At one of the recitals, attended by her parents, Jacqueline was chosen to do a solo. Her father and mother watched

with pride as she went smartly through the paces of
Golliwog's Cakewalk by the French composer, Claude
Debussy. A storm of applause greeted the conclusion of
the number. Blushing with happiness, Jacqueline took
her bows.

But if there was triumph, there was also tragedy. The
year 1940, in which she turned eleven, was a mixture of
both. It was the year she scored her great double win as a
rider at Madison Square Garden. It was the year she discovered a romantic novel of the South—*Gone With the
Wind*—which she read and re-read three times. It was
also the sad, windblown year in which her parents were
divorced.

Growing Up

CHAPTER TWO

Janet and Jack Bouvier's divorce drew Jacqueline and her sister Lee closer together. Before that the girls had been more or less rivals. Their temperaments were so different that it had been hard for them to find a common meeting ground. But their parents' separation changed all that. All at once they found a special need for each other. They sought each other out for comfort and began to share confidences. It was the beginning of a new stage in both their young lives. Intimacy grew into warmth, and then into lasting friendship.

The girls and their mother moved out of the Park Avenue home to a new apartment. The new place was much smaller than the spacious duplex they had left behind. It had one advantage, though. It was close by The Chapin School, where both sisters were enrolled. Though it was a wrench for them to be parted from their beloved father, they adjusted loyally to the situation.

Besides, they continued to see a good deal of Jack Bouvier, who spent as much time with his daughters as the terms of the divorce permitted. Every Sunday he came calling and took them off with him for a day's whirlwind outing. They also stayed with him six weeks of every summer, and half of every other school vacation. So the handsome, dashing figure of John Vernou Bouvier III did not go out of their lives altogether.

Jacqueline would remember these days and all the exciting good times that went with them. A Sunday visit from her father would begin with a series of toots on his automobile horn—a secret signal which only he and the girls shared. Then off they would go to practically anywhere. No one ever knew with Jack Bouvier.

They might go out to colorful Belmont Park to watch the races, where he would let them meet the famous jockeys he knew. Or they might unexpectedly find themselves in the vast reaches of Baker's Field and sit through a lively practice session of the Columbia University baseball team. Or they might take in a movie, with a meal at a Schrafft's restaurant afterward, followed by as many sodas as they could drink.

But whatever it turned out to be, it was always fun, and filled with gaiety and laughter.

He was a thoughtful man, too. The girls couldn't keep a dog in the new apartment because it was too small. So Jack Bouvier made a special arrangement with some local pet shops: the girls were free to go into any one of them at any time, pick up a couple of dogs, and take them for a romp in Central Park. It was this kind of thing that endeared him so to them.

One day, during one of their stays with him, he took them to the New York Stock Exchange. Their father worked in the midst of this hustling, bustling world where fortunes were made and lost in minutes, and to this day Jacqueline remembers the incredible scene from the Exchange gallery. It was a riot of movement and sound that imprinted itself in her mind forever.

Jack Bouvier did not marry again. To the day of his death in 1957 he remained a man who had been married to just one woman in his lifetime. During all the years following his divorce, his girls continued to be the apples of his eye. He followed their ups and downs from a distance but he was always there if they needed him.

In 1942 a new man entered into the lives of the Bouvier girls. This was Hugh D. Auchincloss, their mother's second husband. The marriage took place in June of that year, shortly before Jacqueline's thirteenth birthday. Janet Bouvier was not a Roman Catholic like her first husband, but an Episcopalian, so that she was free to marry again if she wished.

No stepfather could ever replace Jack Bouvier in the girls' affections. But Hugh Auchincloss came awfully close. "A wonderful stepfather," Jacqueline called him. He was all that and more.

From the day they moved into his summer place, Hammersmith Farm, outside of Newport, he made them feel warmly at home. Soon they were exploring its seventy-five acres and getting to know and love every inch of it. There was also Merrywood, the Auchincloss winter estate. Its Georgian architecture gave it a classic air of dignity and grace. From its lofty setting in woods high along the Virginia side of the Potomac, one could look out across the river toward Washington, D.C. on the other side. Here, too, the girls found a world they came to know and love. Forty-six acres were theirs to roam as they pleased. They could also swim in its pool, play badminton or tennis on its courts, or wander down to the stables for a ride on a favorite horse.

It was a perfect place for young people to grow up.

Three other children shared the premises with them, the offspring of a previous marriage by "Uncle Hugh." They also made Jacqueline and Lee feel welcome. There were two boys, Hugh, Jr. and Tommy, and a girl, Nini. Hugh, Jr.—known as "Yusha"—was the eldest. He and Jacqueline soon became fast friends. Later two other children would be born to Janet and Hugh Auchincloss, Jacqueline's half-sister, Janet, and her half-brother, Jamie.

The marriage was a success. The children got along well together. They not only liked each other, they also liked their respective stepparents. Janet tried hard to be a mother to *all* the children, no matter whose they were. She obviously was, for as one of her stepchildren later said about her, "Aunt Janet was really my mother. She did as much for us as she did for her own children."

It was in this setting of new home and new family that the rhythm of life picked up again for Jacqueline. There were the idyllic summers at Hammersmith Farm and the hushed, snowed-in loveliness of Merrywood in the winter. New friends, new experiences—all these wrapped themselves around her now like a cocoon to protect her from the bittersweet memories of the recent past.

There was also a new school, Holton-Arms, which she attended in Washingon. A tough but inspiring teacher, Helen Shearman, taught Latin there and, wonder of all wonders, actually made her students learn it! Jacqueline didn't care very much for the way Miss Shearman drove her reluctant scholars but she had to admit that her methods worked. Everything Miss Shearman taught her stayed with her and she acquired a good working knowledge of that so-called "dead" language in spite of herself. It also taught her another lesson—that the learning process doesn't necessarily work best when a teacher is "soft" on her pupils.

As a growing teenager, Jacqueline was not neglecting the social graces. There were more dancing classes and also dances to which the girls were allowed to invite boys as guests. Her big moment came at a Christmas party when she wore a formal evening dress for the first time. Jacqueline, like all girls in their teens, was very self-conscious about her appearance. Her mother had bought her new gold slippers to wear to the party. When she stared at herself in the mirror her feet looked "enormous." She was convinced they were growing by leaps and bounds and that everyone would notice they were oversize. Underneath a picture snapped on that occasion, she wrote: "Jacqueline's first evening dress. This was lovely blue taffeta and I had a pair of gold track shoes and a really chic feather cut."

Jacqueline was fifteen when she began a brand-new school adventure. Miss Porter's School at Farmington, Connecticut, was a famous school for girls. It was founded in 1843 by the sister of Noah Porter, president of Yale University. Only ten girls were in attendance the first year it opened. But its student body and reputation grew with the years. In less than twenty years it was one of the best known schools of its kind in the country.

Even in those days parents paid two hundred dollars a year—a huge sum of money then—to have their daughters "finished" by Miss Porter. When a girl left Miss Porter's she was ready to take her place in the world of society. She had been schooled in all the right things—manners, the social graces, all the dos and don'ts of ladylike behavior. That is the real meaning of the term "finishing school." For almost a hundred years after its founding Miss Porter's School paid little attention to scholarship. Its girls, aged between fourteen and eighteen, got no formal preparation for college. If they had an interest in scholarship—which was rare—they had to go somewhere else to get it. But all that was changed shortly before Jacqueline arrived there. More emphasis was put on studies. Good teachers were brought in to set up a sound educational program. Now a girl was to be trained for brains as well as beauty, so that she would be ready for Smith or Vassar or any other college she chose after graduating from Miss Porter's.

One of the oldest American institutions of its kind, Miss Porter's is rich with tradition. It also seems to inspire fierce loyalty in its former pupils. Many girls who go there today occupy the same rooms that their mothers and grandmothers did. Physically, nothing much has changed about the school. There are the same buildings, the same familiar landmarks, and in some cases the same furnishings.

There are seven dormitory houses where the girls live, two to a room, in large, cheerful chambers. Every room has bright, gaily-patterned wallpaper that is supposed to set a friendly, congenial tone for its occupants. Although the touch is obvious, it is not artificial, and the girls find their quarters exceedingly pleasant to live in. Each dormitory also has a housemother in charge, a kind, understanding lady who acts as a good shepherd for the girls in her care. When a girl has a male caller, she becomes a chaperon. When a girl has troubles, she lends a willing ear. And when a girl has secrets to confide, she is tight-lipped and trustworthy.

Miss Porter's School believes that girls should become self-reliant. So they do all kinds of odd jobs for themselves, like waiting on tables, at which they take turns. Boys—mostly from Yale and Harvard—are allowed to come up to see the older girls. There is a precise routine to this sort of thing. Two in the afternoon is the scheduled arriving time for male visitors. After a few social hours, they are served tea at the headmaster's house, and then leave very promptly and very suddenly. Few would dare—or want to—break this visiting rule, which has also become a tradition.

Jacqueline liked it at Miss Porter's. One of the first things she found out was that a girl could keep a horse at the stables if she was willing—and able—to pay the twenty-five dollars a month fee. Jacqueline thought it a marvelous opportunity to bring Donny—her beloved Danseuse—along. She asked her family to finance the mare's upkeep. They tried to discourage her by refusing but Jacqueline persisted. Finally she sent off a letter to Grandfather Bouvier, always so understanding in these matters. Would he, please, foot the bill so that Donny could stay with her in Connecticut? Back came a reply from the kindly old gentleman. Yes, he would. Jacqueline was beside herself with happiness. Grandfather Bouvier was an absolute darling. You could always count on him in a pinch.

It snowed early that winter, lots of snow, and she and Donny had a real time of it. Jacqueline found an old sleigh lying around that hadn't been used for years. She got permission to use it and soon she was out there training the clever mare to pull it. Donny got the idea fast after first being tried out on a metal trash can filled with rocks. That winter the sight of Jacqueline driving Donny through the snow became a familiar one in Farmington. Later she put the chestnut through the same treatment with a four-wheel buggy and carried that off successfully, too.

Danseuse lived for twenty years. She had been a champion and then a family pet all that time. Jacqueline really grieved when she died and put together a story of her life in pictures. She wrote: "Danseuse was a family horse and every child had a ride on her. She was such a lady. Her coat glinted in the sun when she was brushed and shining. She knew how lovely she was and flicked her tiny feet out in front of her as she trotted. There was a soft, pink spot at the end of her nose and she would snuffle softly when she knew you had an apple for her." They were loving words written by someone who had lost a dear friend.

Life at Farmington was all Jacqueline could have hoped or asked for. She had Danseuse. The girls were friendly and lots of fun. She liked her teachers and her schoolwork. She had a peach of a first roommate, Sue Norton, and after her, Nancy Tuckerman, whom she liked just as much or better. It helped, of course, that "Tucky's" family and hers were old friends.

It was also nice to have one of Uncle Hugh's sisters nearby. She was the wife of Wilmarth Lewis, a respected literary scholar who had a way of making literature sound like the most exciting subject in the world. One of Jacqueline's great pleasures was to pore over the many books in the Lewis library. Christmas was bookgiving time as far as the Lewises were concerned and every year Jacqueline got a treasured book or two that always turned out to be just what she had wanted.

Jacqueline was a good student at Farmington. But no matter how well she did she never seemed to be able to please Mr. Johnson, the headmaster. He always seemed to think that Jacqueline could do better and wasn't really working at the top of her bent. This seemed strange to her mother, who thought that her daughter's average grades of A minus were outstanding. But Mr. Johnson knew what he was up to. He was a keen judge of young talent and saw in Jacqueline a potential that she had still not realized. A minus might be very good for lots of other girls, but Jacqueline, he thought, was capable of more.

Every once in a while the mischiefmaker in Jacqueline would crop up again. On a dare, while waiting on tables, she dumped a pie in a teacher's lap. Everyone thought it hilariously funny except the teacher—and the headmaster. She had also worked out a foolproof plan for filching cookies from the kitchen. No one knew how she did it, for the kitchen was off limits to those who didn't work there. Yet just about every Sunday night Jacqueline returned mysteriously with a goodly haul, from which she and Tucky nibbled until it was time to strike again.

Some weekends there were visitors, and most magical of all were the weekends when Jack Bouvier came up to see his daughter. His little girl was turning into a beautiful young lady. He looked at her raven hair and then at the gray in his own and realized that the years were flitting by. He was proud of her in every way, of her grades, of the poems and cartoons she did for the school newspaper, of her acting in the school's theatrical group, The Players, and even of the way she'd taught Donny to pull the sleigh. They played together as a team in tennis tournaments and he went to watch her ride Danseuse at Connecticut horse shows. The Farmington girls found Jack Bouvier irresistible. He'd treat Jacqueline and her friends to lunch at the nearby Elm Tree Inn and let them eat their fill—which was plenty. In recalling these fabulous feasts, his daughter said, "We must have eaten him broke."

Graduation day was exciting but sad. There was a pang in Jacqueline's heart as she left Miss Porter's school behind. All the girls in the graduating class had been written up in the class yearbook. There was a mixture of fun and truth in each of these profiles. This was Jacqueline's:

Favorite Song: Lime House Blues
Always Saying: "Play a Rhumba next"
Most Known For: Wit
Aversion: People who ask if her horse is still alive
Where Found: Laughing with Tucky
Ambition: Not to be a housewife

College and Career

Jacqueline was eighteen. She had now reached the proper age to be formally "introduced" to society. Girls who go through this ritual are said to be making their "debuts" and they are referred to as "debutantes." Jacqueline's debut was made in the summer of 1947.

It was a very unusual one in at least one respect, for her new infant half-brother Jamie shared star billing with her. Guests to the tea given for them at Hammer-smith Farm were invited "To meet Miss Jacqueline Lee Bouvier and Master James Lee Auchincloss." Master James had by then attained the ripe old age of five months. Everyone found it very amusing, and everyone had a very good time, including the two guests of honor. One elderly lady, impressed with Jamie's looks and behavior, declared that he had all the makings of a United States Senator.

A more formal party was scheduled for later that summer at the Clambake Club in Newport. Again Jacqueline shared the evening with someone else, this time with Rose Grosvenor, a sister debutante her own age. Families with girls of debutante age often did this sort of thing. They also split the expenses, which made it easier on daddy when bill-paying time arrived. The Grosvenors and the Auchinclosses were good friends and so were the girls. They set each other off very nicely, too. Rose was blonde, with dimples, Jacqueline dark-haired and deeply tanned.

Glowing and lovely, they stood together meeting the guests. Everyone was nice enough to tell them how pretty they looked. But Jacqueline's sister, Lee, stole the show. She had secretly gotten a dressmaker in town to sew up a strapless pink satin gown for her. When fourteen-year-old Lee made her appearance in this striking creation—after dinner when the younger set was allowed in—every eye zeroed in on her, those of the boys especially.

That dress of Lee's really must have been something. Jacqueline borrowed it later and wore it to good advantage. She was convinced that it helped her win the title of "Debutante of the Year," which was bestowed on her by the famous society columnist, Cholly Knickerbocker.

Wrote Cholly: "America is a country of traditions. Every four years we elect a president. . . . And every year a new Queen of Debutantes is crowned. . . . Queen Deb of the Year is Jacqueline Bouvier, a regal brunette who has the classic features and the daintiness of Dresden porcelain. She has poise, is soft-spoken and intelligent, everything the leading debutante should be. . . . You don't have to read a batch of press clippings to be aware of her qualities."

Jacqueline began to receive a lot of attention and publicity. Reporters wanted interviews. Photographers were always snapping her picture. Jacqueline bore up under the burden good-naturedly. She was, by this time, a student at Vassar, the well-known college for girls at Poughkeepsie, New York. The golden summer had long since ended in a whirl of dances and parties. Now she was busily trying to keep up with both her social life and her schoolwork.

Many of Jacqueline's friends were also at Vassar. That

was mainly why she had picked it. She had scored very high marks in her college board exams and could have gone to practically any college she chose. But she wanted to be with people she knew.

School meant the discipline of study again, but there was no stop to the boys who beat their way up to Poughkeepsie to call on her. It was fun being Deb of the Year, but there were also penalties. There began an endless round of weekend dates. Sometimes it was a boy from Harvard, sometimes one from Yale. Sometimes she managed to fit in a weekend at home in Merrywood. Once in a while there was one with her father in New York City.

Jack Bouvier recognized the handwriting on the wall. One of these days one of these dashing young men would make his beautiful daughter a bride. He didn't want to read her any lectures, but he did want to caution her.

In one of his letters to her, he wrote: "I suppose it won't be long before I lose you to some funny-looking 'gink.' . . . However, perhaps you'll use your head and wait until you're at least twenty-one."

He needn't have worried. His daughter was being besieged by admirers, but she was still a long way from getting married. She was too busy taking in all the experiences coming her way. She was growing up and changing in a way that made her more and more of a mystery to the girls at school. She still made friends easily and joined in all the fun and laughter but something inside her was becoming more alone and removed from the world around her. She was beginning to look beyond college and dates and to wonder what it was that the future held for her.

In spite of the fast-moving social merry-go-round she was riding, she got good grades. A Vassar course in Shakespeare given by Miss Helen Sandison, Jacqueline called "the greatest course I ever had." Miss Sandison was one teacher who really loved the subject she taught. Jacqueline fell completely under her spell, and under the spell of Shakespeare. She read all the great plays and was bewitched by their soaring poetry. *Antony and Cleopatra* was her favorite and she committed huge chunks of it to memory.

The school year ended on a note of anticipation. She was looking forward to her first trip abroad. That summer she and three girl friends set out for Europe. One of her past teachers from Holton-Arms, Helen Shearman, went along to chaperon them. The journey across on the *Queen Mary* didn't go nearly fast enough for them. They couldn't wait for the ship to dock. There was a garden party waiting for them at Buckingham Palace. The stepfather of two sisters who were traveling with her was a high official in the American government. It had been he who had wangled the coveted invitation to the party.

It rained cats and dogs when they got there but they hardly minded a bit. There was a crush of people among whom they wandered, constantly looking for important faces. They never did get to meet King George VI and his wife Queen Elizabeth, but they walked right over to Winston Churchill who was very nice about it and shook all their hands.

That marked the social high point of their European tour. There was nothing to equal it for excitement and elegance, but there were lots of other places they got to see during the six weeks they were on the move. After England they had a look at Paris and the French country-side. Then it was on to Switzerland and the history-drenched cities of Italy. From Rome they went back to Paris for a brief fling before starting back for home.

Vassar in the fall was lovely but it was no match for Jacqueline's summer memories of Europe. She had fallen in love with the old continent, especially Paris, and couldn't wait to get back again. When she found out that Smith College girls could spend their junior year at a foreign university she made up her mind to go to France. That meant switching from Vassar, so she did. Although there were special requirements for girls who wanted to join such groups, Jacqueline made the grade easily. It meant boning up on her French, but by the time summer had rolled around she was ready for the big adventure.

It began with a summer session at the University of
Grenoble. On the way there—at the train station in
Paris—she got very special treatment from a porter who
found out that her name was the same as his daughter's.
He couldn't seem to do enough for her and shook her
hand warmly over and over again before her bus pulled
out of the station.

At Grenoble she lived with a French family. Not too
far away was the town from which her Bouvier ancestor
had emigrated. When she had free time she went on
sightseeing tours that were never long enough to satisfy
her endless curiosity. Her letters home were full of poetic
touches about the places she saw and visited. When summer drew to a close she was sorry to leave.

The Sorbonne in Paris is one of the most famous uni-
versities in the world. It was in this historic institution of
learning, founded way back in the year 1256, that Jacqueline was to study for a year. She arrived in Paris in the
autumn of 1949. Again she went to live with a French
family. She could have stayed at the regular dormitory
set aside for American students but she wanted to be
where French was spoken all the time so she could really
learn it.

The Comtesse de Renty was a widow who took in
student boarders to make ends meet. She had two daughters and a grandson who lived with her. Jacqueline and

two other American girls were paying guests. This made for a total of seven people living together in the de Renty apartment. All seven shared the one bathroom and its old tin bathtub. There was supposed to be hot water from a water heater but it didn't work too well. Jacqueline even had it blow up on her right in the middle of a bath!

It was cold that winter in Paris and the apartment had no heat. When Emile Zola was a struggling young writer living in a cold Paris flat, he used to wrap himself up in sweaters and blankets and anything else that was handy while he wrote the stories that eventually made him famous. Jacqueline had to do pretty much the same thing in order to get through her homework. It didn't help much even though she cuddled up in bed wearing mittens and earmuffs.

Roughing it like this in Paris hadn't been part of Jacqueline's plans but she took it all in stride. Not a whimper or a murmur of complaint passed her lips. Not a word about it found its way into her letters. When Janet and Hugh Auchincloss visited her at the Comtesse's that winter they discovered for the first time the harsh conditions under which she had been living and studying. Neither of them made a fuss about it. Instead they were proud of her for not complaining.

At the Sorbonne Jacqueline took courses in French civilization and literature. She was also getting to know a different kind of Paris from the one she had visited the year before. Then she had gone to all the well-known places that tourists go to because they have glamorous reputations. Now she began to know Paris from the inside. She went to wonderful cafes and small, out-of-the-way restaurants. She went to museums and looked open-mouthed at the great pictures which up to then she had seen only in art books. She went to the theater and to the opera and to marvelous performances of ballet that fairly took her breath away. She took long walks along the Seine and knew the strange shadowed loveliness of Paris in the rain. And she was learning French from the Comtesse and her family in a way that she could never have learned it in class.

When it came time to set sail for home at the end of the school year, Jacqueline felt sad. Leaving Paris was like turning her back on an old and dear friend. But it wasn't too long before she was back in the swim of things at Hammersmith Farm, exploring once again on foot and horseback the rolling green farm country that in the summer looked as if an artist had painted it there.

It was peaceful and serene at Hammersmith. Time seemed to have no meaning there. It was like one long lazy summer day that suddenly melted away and became autumn. Then it was time for school again. The scene shifted to the crispness of a new season at Merrywood.

There was always a different feeling at Merrywood, a tingle in the air that set the blood to racing. The winding days of autumn and the white stretch of winter lay ahead. It would be a time for doing. It would also be a time for planning and wondering. This was to be Jacqueline's last year at college. What was to come after it?

She had decided to stay close to home this year, so she enrolled at George Washington University which was conveniently nearby in Washington, D.C. She had another reason for making the change. Jacqueline had been idly turning over in her mind the possibility of going into newspaper or magazine work, and the local university had a good course in journalism.

In line with this she decided to enter *Vogue* magazine's yearly contest for senior college girls. There was an enticing prize—it was called the *Prix de Paris*—for the winner, a staff job with *Vogue* for a whole year. Six months of this period would be spent with its Paris publication, the remaining six months with the American one in New York.

The contest was far from easy. It had some tough, brain-twisting requirements. She had to write a series of papers on fashion and work up, in detail, her ideas for a complete issue of *Vogue*. She also had to write a 1,500-word short story and a 500-word essay with the title, "People I Wish I Had Known." Jacqueline was most intrigued by the essay. She chose two famous writers and a ballet impressario for the people she wished she had known. They were very unusual, to say the least. The two writers were Oscar Wilde, an Irishman, and the French poet, Charles Baudelaire. The ballet impressario, Serge Diaghilev was a Russian. It was a most surprising trio for an American girl—especially one of her age—to have selected.

Although she worked very hard on the contest, Jacqueline never dreamed she would win. Early in 1951 the winner was announced: Jacqueline Lee Bouvier, a senior at George Washington University. No one was more surprised by the outcome than Jacqueline. She was also very pleased. It was most flattering to have won out over the 1,280 other girls who had competed for the first prize.

Now Jacqueline had another problem—whether or not to accept the prize. It would be fun to work on a big, important magazine like Vogue—especially in Paris. But her mother thought otherwise. Janet Bouvier did not want her daughter to go back to Paris. She felt that the year Jacqueline had already spent there was enough and that another long stay in the enchanted French city might turn her daughter into a real bohemian. She also thought it important that Jacqueline stay on at the university and complete her final college year. Her mother's arguments helped Jacqueline make up her mind. With a twinge of regret, she turned down the *Vogue* job.

There was a consolation prize for her after school was

over. Sister Lee was making her first trip to Europe and Jacqueline went along, too. She was already an old hand at traveling and knew all the ropes. They hired a car in Paris and drove through the French countryside toward the Spanish frontier. All too quickly, it seemed, they had left France behind. Spain was so different it was like shutting the door on the rest of Europe. It had timeless towns and villages that hadn't changed in centuries. If that crazy old knight Don Quixote had suddenly showed up and challenged the metal monster they were driving to a duel they wouldn't have been at all surprised. Saying good-bye to Spain was like saying good-bye to the past.

Italy was next, and in the city of Florence, that lovely flower of Italian culture, Jacqueline turned twenty-two. It was in Florence too—just outside the city—that she made a pilgrimmage to the home of the great art critic, Bernard Berenson. The visit and their talk together made a deep impression on her. Berenson was already a very old man in his late eighties when Jacqueline saw him. He lived to the age of ninety-four and died in 1959. The world's greatest expert on Italian renaissance painting was very gracious to the two Bouvier girls. This man of immense learning and culture was one of Jacqueline's idols. Only one other great man she was to meet ever impressed her as much—General Charles de Gaulle.

Even though she had refused the Paris job with *Vogue,*

Jacqueline still had journalistic ambitions. This time, though, she had her eyes on the newspapers. Arthur Krock, the noted columnist for the New York *Times,* was a family friend. He also knew everyone there was to know in Washington and had a lot of influence. One of those he knew very well was Frank Waldrop, the editor of the Washington *Times-Herald.* One day, late in 1951, he called him on the telephone.

Waldrop was used to getting calls from people he knew asking for jobs for friends and relatives. Usually he turned a deaf ear to such requests. But Krock was different. He respected Krock and knew that he wouldn't make recommendations lightly. So when Krock said he had a talented prospect for him, Waldrop opened both ears wide.

"I have a wonder for you," said Krock. "She's round-eyed, clever, and wants to go into journalism. Will you see her?"

"Sure," said Waldrop. "Send her around."

Jacqueline went to see him just before Christmastime. Waldrop liked what he saw. She was pretty, intelligent, and seemed in dead earnest, a very good combination. She certainly didn't need the $42.50 a week that the job paid, but he wouldn't hold that against her. He told her to report back after the holidays—the job was hers.

Nineteen fifty-two was just getting under way when

Jacqueline started her newspaper career. At first, just to get her feet wet, she was sent out on routine assignments. A young girl reporter covering police courts and emergency wards of hospitals gets to see some pretty unsettling sights. Jacqueline didn't bat an eyelash—at least outwardly. But she probably didn't relish the idea of doing it on a regular basis. She needn't have worried, for Waldrop had other, more interesting, plans for her.

The *Times-Herald* had an "Inquiring Photographer" column which it ran regularly. The feature had a simple but very appealing format. A reporter was sent out to ask people questions and to report their answers and opinions. The questions covered a wide range of subjects. Some were serious, some were humorous. A typical question might be, "Are senators' salaries too high or too low?"—or "Should a tall woman marry a short man?" Those interviewed had their pictures as well as their answers printed in the newspaper. They might be just ordinary people—the so-called "man in the street"—or they might be celebrities. The column had long been one of the paper's most popular attractions. It had also always been written by a man. Waldrop now decided on a new course. He changed the name of the column to the *Inquiring Camera Girl* and gave the assignment to Jacqueline.

The new Inquiring Camera Girl found herself suddenly very busy. She had to interview eight or ten people for each column. She also had to snap their pictures and then go back to the office and write the column. At first she had a little difficulty with the picture-taking part of it. She had told Waldrop that she knew how to use a camera—which she did. It turned out, however, that the camera in question—a professional model—was vastly different from the ones Jacqueline was accustomed to working with. She immediately signed up for a course at a photography school. Soon she was making expert use of the heavy Graflex she had to lug around with her.

Waldrop liked his new Camera Girl. He found her efficient and hardworking. She did her job well and rarely complained. He was getting his money's worth and he knew it. There was a lot of leg work involved in being the Inquiring Camera Girl for a big newspaper. Pretty quickly Jacqueline knew her way around every nook and cranny of the nation's capital. She was getting to know it and it was certainly getting to know her. The Inquiring Camera Girl was a big hit with her readers.

At first Jacqueline's name did not appear with her column. In newspaper terms this is called a "by-line." Jacqueline had to earn her by-line first, the hard way, by working for it and deserving it. After several months editor Waldrop decided that the big day had arrived. On March 26, 1952, *Times-Herald* readers learned for the first time that the name of the Inquiring Camera Girl was Jacqueline Lee Bouvier.

Jacqueline enjoyed doing the column. She also liked making up the questions she asked people. It gave her lots of opportunity to use her imagination and humor. Many of the replies she got to her questions were unusual. Actor James Stewart, for instance, was asked if he had a secret ambition. He had—a most surprising one. He had always wanted to be a circus clown! Another time she asked a group of women, "Which First Lady would you liked to have been?" One woman's answer—read today—makes strange and chilling reading. She said: "Lincoln's. I could have prevented the assassination. He was tired that night and I wouldn't have let him go to the theater. I always thought that if I'd been his wife I'd have prevented his death."

Above all, Jacqueline liked to interview children because, as she said, "they make the best stories." She found them the easiest to talk to. They were also frank, often to the point of embarrassment.

One day she interviewed little Patricia Nixon, then six years old, the daughter of Richard Nixon. It was right after the 1952 elections and Senator Nixon had just been elected Vice-President. Jacqueline's question was: "What do you think of Senator Nixon now?" Little Tricia, as she was called, made no bones about the way she felt. Said she: "He's always away. If he's famous why can't he stay at home. See this picture? That's a coming home present I made for Daddy. Julie did one too, but she can't color as well as me. All my class was voting for Eisenhower, but I told them I was just going to vote for Daddy."

Not long after this there was another amusing interview with the younger set. This time it was with two nieces of the new President, Dwight Eisenhower, whom everyone called "Ike." Jacqueline wanted to know if their lives had changed in any way since their uncle had become President. One of the girls, aged eleven, thought it might have some effect on her career as a baby-sitter. "I've been charging fifty cents an hour," she said. "Now that my uncle is President of the United States, don't you think I should get seventy-five?"

She also told Jacqueline what her friends at school thought: "A girl in my class said that when my uncle's President, I should tell the teacher to give me good marks or he'd throw her off the school board. But you know, I don't think that would do me any good, because if Uncle Ike heard that, he'd tell my mother and would she get mad!"

Needless to say, *Times-Herald* readers found such interviews very much to their tastes. So did editor Waldrop, who encouraged her to do more of the same.

Jacqueline was usually on her own in gathering material for her column, but sometimes Waldrop had suggestions to make. One day he summoned her to his office. There was a special twinkle in his eye as he spoke. He had an assignment he knew she would particularly enjoy. He wanted her to journey up to Capitol Hill for an interview with a brand-new senator who had just made the big jump from the House of Representatives to the Senate. The new Senator's name was John Fitzgerald Kennedy.

Waldrop chuckled as he sent her on her way. He knew something that few other people knew. His Inquiring Camera Girl had been seen occasionally in the company of young Kennedy. There were even rumors that they were dating each other secretly. "Don't get your hopes up," he called out after her. "He's too old for you. Besides, he doesn't want to get married."

Jacqueline pretended she hadn't heard. She didn't want to let on that Waldrop had hit home with his remarks. She had indeed been seeing Senator Kennedy— and more often than Waldrop or anyone else imagined. As for the young Senator not being the marrying kind, that had certainly been true in the past. But Jacqueline had good reason to suspect that the handsome thirty-five-year-old lawmaker might not remain single much longer.

Courtship and Marriage

John F. Kennedy was the most eligible bachelor in Congress. At least that's what everyone said he was, including the press, his colleagues, and all the pining young ladies who had set their caps for him. He was rich and good-looking. He was a war hero who had survived an incredible sea adventure in the Pacific and had a shiny medal to show for it. He also had a bright political future ahead of him. He had just won a sensational victory in the 1952 elections. Now his star blazed more brilliantly than ever in the political heavens. Some even said—after this triumph—that he had his future sights set on the Presidency. It was not widely known, however, that he also had his sights set on the *Times-Herald*'s Inquiring Camera Girl.

The romance between Jacqueline and young Kennedy had had a hard time getting off the ground. Their paths had first crossed in 1948, back in the days when the lovely young debutante was making male hearts flutter on practically every Ivy League campus. Both had been guests at a Long Island wedding where the bride that day was the sister of a mutual friend, Charles Bartlett. They were both too busy making the rounds and talking to other people to ever get a chance to talk to each other for more than a polite sentence or two. Three years were to pass before they met again.

In all that time Charles Bartlett was doing his level best to trap them into a meeting. Newspaperman Bartlett, a good friend of both, kept up a barrage of matchmaking propaganda. When he saw Jacqueline he praised Kennedy; when he saw Kennedy he praised Jacqueline. Bartlett was convinced that if they ever got together they would hit it off like a dream. He was almost right.

The long-hoped-for meeting finally came about. On a

hot night in June, 1951, eight people sat down to dinner at the Bartlett home in Georgetown. Two of them were Jacqueline Bouvier and John Kennedy. At first everything seemed to go swimmingly. The two had no difficulty in making table talk. Soon they were calling each other by their nicknames, Jackie and Jack. They even laughed at each other's joking remarks, a good sign from Bartlett's point of view.

After dinner there was more pleasant talk in the garden. When it came time to go, Kennedy, in high good humor, walked Jacqueline to her car which was parked outside. He was in the middle of asking for a date when there was a commotion in Jacqueline's car. The Bartletts' dog, who had been trotting along in front of them, had made a sudden leap into the back seat and come down smack in someone's lap. The mysterious passenger in the back seat, it turned out, was one of Jacqueline's current boy friends. Completely by chance he had been passing by the Bartlett house and spotted Jacqueline's car. He had thought it would be a big joke to sit there in the back seat and surprise her when she came out. It was a big surprise all the way around. More jolted than anyone was Congressman Kennedy. He suddenly had the feeling that he was an unwelcome third party. Muttering good night, he beat a swift retreat.

Poor Charles Bartlett was completely downcast. He

had been so sure of everything, and now this had happened. Sadly he decided that one could do so much and no more. If Jacqueline and Jack Kennedy were ever to get together they would have to do so on their own. They did just that, but it took almost a year before they picked up the pieces of that ill-fated June night at the Bartletts'.

Jacqueline and John Kennedy went their separate ways. That very same summer the Bouvier sisters took their European tour together. Later that year Jacqueline began putting out feelers for a newspaper job. She got the job with the *Times-Herald*. She also became engaged, briefly, to John G. W. Husted, Jr. of New York.

Young Husted's father was a prominent New York banker. He himself was in the investment business as a stockbroker. During World War II, as a marine, he had seen service in both Europe and India. People who knew them both thought it a sound, sensible match. The engagement announcement was made in the *Times-Herald* on January 21, 1952. The wedding was set for some time in June.

It was obvious from the start that Jacqueline hadn't been exactly swept off her feet. Somewhere along the way she began to have second thoughts. As winter moved toward spring the ties binding her to Husted began to weaken. By April they were severed altogether. The engagement was broken "by mutual consent."

In the meantime, John Kennedy had come back into

her life. They had met again in the natural course of things when the Inquiring Camera Girl went poking around Capitol Hill looking for a story. Among the lawmakers holding forth there in the halls of Congress was young Mr. Kennedy. He remembered Jacqueline all too well, but he was more than willing to forgive and forget. This time they didn't need Charles Bartlett to make their social arrangements. They made their own. On their first date they went dancing. Fortunately there was no third party around to pop up suddenly like a jack-in-the-box, so the evening went beautifully. After that there were many more dates. They stayed away from public places, though. Tongues would start wagging quickly if it got out that John Kennedy was squiring that attractive girl reporter around town.

The political pace picked up again for Kennedy in the summer and fall. He had very little time to spare for dates and courting. He was running for the Senate against Henry Cabot Lodge, a very tough opponent. Lodge was favored to win, but Kennedy seemed to relish the position of underdog. It made him redouble his efforts.

Between speeches in Massachusetts he managed to sneak a few moments for phone calls to Jacqueline. Sometimes he even squeezed in a quick plane flight just to see her and take her out to a movie.

After he won his race for the Senate, Jack Kennedy

went back to wooing the fair Miss Bouvier on a regular basis. Still wanting to avoid publicity, they often took refuge with friends. They were regular visitors at the Bartletts', who were only too delighted to give them sanctuary. For Charles Bartlett the romance was a personal kind of triumph. It proved that he wasn't such a bad matchmaker after all.

Bobby and Ethel Kennedy, Jack's brother and sister-in-law, also provided shelter on occasion, as did others they knew and trusted. Then there was always the movies. Kennedy liked fast-moving, action-filled films, especially those about the West and the Civil War. Jacqueline's tastes ran more to foreign films. They compromised. She sat bravely through his westerns and action dramas; he suffered and wriggled and writhed his way through the foreign ones.

Rarely were there any private moments together for them. The only times they were really alone was when he drove her home to Merrywood in the evening. There were many such nights, and soon he could have driven the way blindfolded on the familiar route that led along the Potomac and then across the Key Bridge into Virginia.

It was a hectic period that kept them both on the run. They saw a lot of each other but their meetings always had the feeling of hurry and schedule. The winter of

1953 turned to spring and Jack Kennedy had still not popped the question. Early in May Jacqueline got a phone call from a girl named Aileen Bowdoin, one of the two sisters with whom she had made her first trip to Europe. Aileen was going to London to see the coronation of Queen Elizabeth. Would Jacqueline like to go along? The *Queen Mary* would be sailing in two days. Jacqueline made a fast decision. Maybe a little absence would make a certain heart grow fonder. She said, yes, she would go. Two days later she was aboard ship and on her way.

Editor Waldrop had no objection to her going. He even put her on special assignment. While she was there she could cover the coronation for the *Times-Herald*. It turned out well for both of them. Jacqueline's stories, filed from London, were filled with the warmth, color and excitement of the great occasion. She also did amusing little line drawings that appeared with her articles. Both the sketches and the reports—among the best she wrote—were a great success.

Jack Kennedy thought they were good, too. "Articles excellent," he wired her, "but you are missed." And she *was*. He proved how much when he got word that her homebound plane would land in Boston before flying on to New York. When the two girls, Jacqueline and Aileen, strolled into the lounge of the Boston airport there was the tall, lean Senator waiting to greet them. From the impatient look of him it was plain to see that he had something important on his mind. That very day, when they were alone, he asked her to marry him. It was a perfect coming-home present for Jacqueline. She had two presents for him. One was her answer to his proposal— Yes! The other was a suitcase full of books on politics which she'd picked up for him in little out-of-the-way London bookshops. He gratefully accepted both.

Then he told her, with a wry look, that they would have to hold off their engagement announcement until later that month. The *Saturday Evening Post* was due out shortly with an article about him. He didn't want to spoil its sales. They both roared with laughter when he told her the title of the article: "Jack Kennedy—the Senate's Gay Young Bachelor."

The article appeared without mishap. The *Saturday Evening Post* sold lots of copies. Readers read for the last time about the elusive Jack Kennedy who had so far kept out of the clutches of designing females. They were left with the feeling that it would be many a moon before Mr. Kennedy allowed himself to be lured into the treacherous byways of matrimony. Right on the heels of this exclusive inside story—on June 25—the same readers learned through their newspapers that bachelor Kennedy had bitten the dust. The villain of the piece—the wily

huntress who had brought him down—was, of all things,
a society girl turned newspaperwoman. Never before in
the history of male versus female had bachelorhood
ended so swiftly after having been so widely advertised.
Official Washington was stunned, but it was also amused.

As for Jacqueline, she was just plain happy. She turned
in her resignation to editor Waldrop who was genuinely
sorry to see his Inquiring Camera Girl reach the end of
the journalistic trail. She had developed into a good
reporter and a good writer. She would be missed.

She also discovered, very quickly, that the journalistic
shoe was now on the other foot. As a reporter it had been
she who had prowled and snooped around looking for
good stories. Now she herself had become the story. As
the fiancé of Jack Kennedy she was news. They kept
being followed by an endless procession of reporters and
photographers who left them no privacy. Even when she
went sailing with Jack on his sloop there, big as life, was a
photographer from *Life* snapping pictures of them from
all angles.

That summer for Jacqueline was a training course in
being the wife of a politician. It was like being on a tread-
mill that never stopped moving. When Jack went somewhere to make a speech she went along, too. She met his
political friends and associates. Everywhere there were
new people to meet and talk to, fast introductions, the

soft buzz of voices and the polite faces behind them. She learned how to put a smile on her face in public and keep it there, and how to behave and what to say when being interviewed by the clever ladies and gentlemen of the press.

She also got a closer look at the Kennedy family and began to get a feeling of what it would be like to be part of that vast, sprawling clan. It wasn't only a large family —it was *active*. Being with them one could almost feel the electric crackle of energy in the air. This superabundance of vigor—or "vigah," as Jack pronounced it— found its outlet in games and competition that ran all the way from touch football in the afternoon to Monopoly in the evening. Before she knew what was happening, Jacqueline found herself racing across the lawns of the Kennedy homes at Hyannis Port in hot pursuit of a football and the tireless players who tossed, kicked, and ran it back and forth over and over again. It was quite a change from the lazy afternoons at Hammersmith and the quiet sedateness of Merrywood.

Being with the Kennedys was an overwhelming and totally unbelievable experience. The sheer size of the family was impressive. Leaving out the cousins and the aunts and uncles and all the other relatives, there were, to begin with, Jack's two brothers, Bob and Teddy, and Bob's wife, Ethel and their children. Then there were his three sisters, Eunice, Jean, and Pat and their children and respective husbands, Sargent Shriver, Stephen Smith and Peter Lawford, the actor. Heading the list, of course, were Jack's parents, Joseph Patrick Kennedy and Rose Fitzgerald Kennedy.

This was formidable enough all by itself, but when other assorted relations put in their appearance at Hyannis Port, it was like having a close-up look at the population explosion. Jacqueline never quite got used to these enormous get-togethers which were totally different from her own family experience. "Just watching them wore me out," she is once reported to have said.

The elder Kennedy ruled his unruly roost with a mixture of love and an iron hand. He was a man who left no doubt about where he stood on any question. He had a quick temper and an even quicker tongue. Both had often gotten him into hot water. His children might disagree with some of their father's opinions, but they always treated him with respect and deep affection. In the Kennedy world there was but one chief and monarch and his name was Joe Kennedy.

This Irish boy from Boston had known what he wanted right from the very start and gone after it. His rise to riches and fame had a storybook quality to it. He was only in his thirties when he made his first million. But that was just the beginning. When Jacqueline first knew him his wealth was reputed to be in the hundreds of millions and still growing.

In the 1930's he had been one of the first very rich men in the country to support President Franklin Delano Roosevelt. The President later appointed him to high government posts. Just before World War II broke out he became the American Ambassador to England. At one time he'd even had the idea of trying for the Presidency himself. When that ambition was thwarted, Joe Kennedy decided his sons might do better at politics than he had.

Joe Kennedy had made his money and his reputation as a businessman but he had other plans for his sons. Politics—public life—government—that was where he wanted them to make their marks. Besides, business was strictly for making money. He'd already made the money, so there was no need for them to. So the boys got the widest kind of educational background, one that would prepare them for the broad-ranging problems one encountered in public affairs. He sent his two oldest boys, Joe, Jr. and Jack, to Harvard, his own old alma mater. Later he did the same with the younger ones, Bob and Teddy. Joe, Jr. and Jack also studied at the London School of Economics where they took courses under a famous professor who was also a socialist, Harold Laski. Joe was a firm believer in capitalism and free enterprise but he wasn't afraid of exposing his sons to other influences and ideas. Only in that way, he believed, would they ever get to know what the world was really like.

His hopes had first rested on his oldest son, Joseph P. Kennedy, Jr. This handsome, brilliant boy was a sure bet to make a name for himself. Then World War II came along. Joe, Jr. joined the Navy and became a naval pilot. Jack, the next oldest, also went with the Navy. The other two boys, Bob and Teddy, were still too young to serve. It didn't take long for tragedy to strike.

First Jack, the skipper of a PT boat, had his craft rammed and sliced in half by a Japanese destroyer. He was reported lost at sea. Days passed and still there was no word. Joe Kennedy had been informed by the Navy Department that his son was missing. He didn't tell his wife because he was sure the boy would show up somewhere. Five days later Jack was found. He had spent exhausting long hours in the water swimming back and forth between islands. His back was practically broken in half and he was barely alive. But he was alive and safe. Only then did Joe tell his wife what had happened.

Next time Joe and Rose Kennedy weren't so lucky. Again a son was reported missing in action, this time pilot Joe, Jr. He had flown on a special bombing mission across the English Channel, for which he had volunteered. His plane was reported to have blown up mysteriously in mid-air. Joe Kennedy refused to believe his son was dead. He *couldn't* be dead. He had so many plans for him. It took weeks, months, even years before the reality sank in, and he could accept it.

The war took still further toll of the Kennedys. Daughter Kathleen, next to the oldest of the girls, had also felt the call to duty. In 1944 she joined the Red Cross and was sent to London. There she met and fell in love with an English nobleman, the Marquess of Hartington. They were married in the spring of that year. Four months later the Marquess was dead, killed in action in France. Kathleen decided to stay in England and make it her home, as it had been her husband's. On May 13, 1948, she herself met death in a plane crash in southern France.

Another family sorrow was not too well known. The oldest daughter, Rosemary, had been a retarded child. For years her father and mother kept her at home, hoping and praying that she would get well. But the years only saw a steady decline in her condition. She was finally sent to live and to be cared for at a Catholic institution in Wisconsin.

These were misfortunes enough for three families, and they left their scars. But the Kennedys were a tightly knit group. They found solace and comfort in each other. Joe Kennedy had taught his children a stern code of life, that the race went to those who competed the hardest.

There was a time for tears, but life had to go on. When
you got knocked down you had to pick yourself up off the
floor and fight even harder.

The death of Joe, Jr. had been an especially severe
blow to his father. He had counted on young Joe to bring
luster to the family name in the field of politics. Now the
gap he had left would have to be filled by the son next in
line—Jack.

Jack Kennedy hadn't really wanted to go into politics.
His tastes ran more to writing or teaching. In his
twenties, just before World War II, he had written a
book called *Why England Slept*. It was an astonishing
work to have come from the pen of one so young and
drew a good deal of critical praise. Most people thought
that Jack might wind up a journalist or an historian
or a lawyer. But his brother's death changed all that. He
was next in line and Joe, Sr. told him it was his duty to
take Joe, Jr.'s place. To please his father he took his first
plunge into politics.

In 1946 war-hero Kennedy was elected to the United
States Congress. He was twenty-nine years old. It was the
beginning of a speedy rise to the top. As he learned the
political ropes, Jack learned something else, too. He
liked politics. He also found that he had a natural talent
for it.

The Kennedy campaigns became famous because they

were so different. Jack might be the candidate but he had the devoted help of every member of the family. Each campaign was, in the truest sense of the word, a family affair. Brothers and brothers-in-law, sisters and sisters-in-law—all pitched in when Jack was up for election. Even mother Rose Kennedy, a modest, retiring woman, took to the stump to tell voters to cast their ballots for her son. Other women in other families might stay out of the political line of fire, but not the Kennedy women. They marched right into the thick of battle, and actually seemed to like it. Only Joe Kennedy, a controversial figure, stayed discreetly in the background.

This, then, was the family that Jacqueline would soon be joining. Becoming a Kennedy was like being admitted to a very exclusive private club. There were special privileges but there were also strong obligations. It was one for all and all for one, just like the Three Musketeers of Alexandre Dumas who were sworn together into a blood brotherhood. Already she had an inkling of what she would have to face both privately and publicly. It would take time before she learned to fit in. But she was willing to try—even to play touch football if she had to.

While Jacqueline was trying her best to survive the summer, arrangements were being made for the wedding, which was to be held on September 12, 1953, at St. Mary's Church in Newport, Rhode Island. After the ceremony there would be a reception at Hammersmith Farm.

The celebrating got off to an early start. Jack's father and mother threw a marathon party at Hyannis Port. It began five days before the wedding and lasted for four. The famous Kennedy vitality was on full display as the helpless guests were caught up in a whirlwind of activities. They played endless sets of tennis. They emerged winded and often wounded from scrimmages of touch football. They swam, they sailed, they hiked. They even went on picnics. When evening came and quiet settled over other parts of the land, there was still no rest at the Kennedy's. A scavenger hunt continued far into the night, topped off by a session of charades before the worn-out celebrants were allowed to sneak off to bed and a few hours of blessed sleep. Their escape was a brief one. In the morning, bright and early, the same incredible program began all over again.

Jack seemed to be enjoying every action-filled moment. He was an ardent touch football player, as were all the Kennedys, including the girls. He enjoyed the roughhouse and competition and played to win. When they held sailboat races he was all business as he piloted his old 24-footer, the *Victura,* to a succession of victories. Being with his family was like catnip to the Senator. Jacqueline had never seen him so happy and relaxed.

The four days of fun and games was a grueling experience for all but the Kennedys. Everyone else was willing to call it quits long before the party ended. They were ready to drop when it finally did. The Kennedys were ready, willing and able to go on for four more. Or forty, if need be.

But first they had a brother to get married. The whole group—family and friends—moved its base of operations to Newport. There, on the night before the wedding, Jacqueline and Jack were the guests of honor at a bridal dinner given by Janet and Hugh Auchincloss at the Clambake Club. Jack made a humorous speech about his reasons for marrying. Jacqueline had been too clever a reporter and knew all his political secrets. Therefore, the only way he could protect himself was to marry her.

Jacqueline also made a speech. Her husband-to-be, she said, was noted as a man of letters. But he would never rank very high as a writer of romantic letters. To the delight of everyone present, she held up a single postcard which Jack had once sent her from Bermuda. Outside of his cablegram to her in England, it was the only "letter" she had ever gotten from him during their courtship. It read: "Wish you were here. Jack."

September twelfth was a day bright with sunlight. Strong gusts of wind blew the first brown-specked leaves from the trees. At St. Mary's Church six hundred guests sat in pin-dropping quiet as Archbishop Cushing of Boston pronounced the rites of marriage. When his sonorous intonation ceased, Jacqueline had become, quite suddenly and magically, Mrs. John Fitzgerald Kennedy.

The rest of the afternoon was a blur of wind and sun and sound in the green gardens of Hammersmith. Just as he had at her mother's wedding twenty-five years ago, Meyer Davis provided the lilting strains of dance music. The hundreds of guests streamed through the house and across the lawns. There was laughter and merrymaking and toasts to the happy future of the bride and groom. And then it was time to go.

Jacqueline slipped away for a moment to change out of her white wedding gown. When she came back to say good-bye she was dressed in a sensible gray suit that looked just right for traveling. She and the Senator had picked Mexico for their honeymoon. Years ago, on a trip there with her mother and stepfather, Jacqueline had seen a house in Acapulco that looked as if it had been specially made for newlyweds. She had never forgotten it. It was in this house, high on a cliff overlooking the sea, that they would spend the first weeks of their marriage.

Like the girl in the fairy tale, the dream of Jacqueline Bouvier had come true. She had met and married the handsome prince. Now their life together—for better or for worse—would begin.

The Story of a Book

Jack Kennedy had a long history of back trouble. He had hurt it for the first time playing football at prep school. The injury had been further aggravated during the war when his boat, PT-109, was hit by a Japanese destroyer and he had been hurled into the water. He had also come down with malaria while serving in the Pacific. Both these ailments came back periodically to plague him after the war.

Several weeks before the wedding he was laid low by a malaria attack. On the day of the wedding his back hurt so much that it was only by gritting his teeth that he had managed to get into a kneeling position during the ceremony. In the summer of 1954 the pain was getting worse. Most of the time the young Senator had to hobble around on crutches. He was reaching a point of decision—whether to remain permanently crippled or to risk an operation that might endanger his life.

It had not been a good first year of married life for either Jacqueline or her husband. All newly married couples go through an initial period of adjustment. The Kennedys did, too.

One of the main troubles was Jack's career as a politician. It kept him away from home much of the time. The lack of a permanent home also had an unsettling influence. They were always on the move, a month or so at Merrywood, several weeks at Hyannis Port, rented apartments, hotels, trips around the country and abroad. They'd barely had time to settle down somewhere before they were off again on another jaunt. It was, as Jacqueline herself described it, "hectic." "I soon learned to pack quickly and go anywhere," she said.

Jacqueline tried hard to make a home for them no matter where they were, but his gypsy way of life kept getting in the way. They seemed always to be at cross purposes. He didn't mind the crowds, the constant traveling, and he loved the hurly-burly pace and excitement of politics. She, on the other hand, preferred to be with small groups of friends and yearned for a house they could really call their own. As for politicians, she could take them or leave them—mostly leave them.

Except for Jack, of course. But she didn't really look upon her husband as a typical politician. He had a fine mind and the temperament and interests of a scholar. This had been one of the things that had attracted her to him in the first place. That, and his wit, which was a side of him that only his close friends knew. Typical politician or not, Jack Kennedy was a complete political animal who lived, breathed and ate politics. The world of power and politics fascinated him and he swam happily about in its turbulent waters. Even when he was at home, politics would get in the way of his relationship with Jacqueline. When he was occupied by a political problem, Jacqueline, as she herself said, "might as well have been in Alaska." It was the not unusual case of the husband who brought his work home from the office. In this instance the work was politics.

She couldn't understand what there was about government and politics that appealed so to Jack. To her, as to most women, the whole thing seemed humdrum. In order to give it a fair chance, she took a course in American history at the Georgetown School of Foreign Service.

Every day, that first winter, she trudged off to class to listen to the instructor unroll the great pageant of the American story. It was all very interesting and very enlightening but it was really not her cup of tea. European history, especially the gilded eighteenth century, with its grace and manners, she found much more congenial. "American history," she concluded, "is for men."

Still, she had learned a lot about it, more than she thought, as it later turned out. It was hard to resist Jack when he got going on the subject. He had such wide knowledge and deep understanding that he made you listen and think in spite of yourself; and he also had a wonderful way of passing along his own enthusiasm. At any rate, he was immensely pleased and flattered—and amused—that she had gone back to school just to find a common meeting ground with him.

He did something for her, too. It had to do with his clothes. Before his marriage the Senator had been overly casual in his wardrobe. He hated to dress up. His favorite getup was a jacket, khaki slacks, and tennis sneakers. Hostesses at dinner parties learned not to look too shocked when young Kennedy showed up in his makeshift outfits. For Jacqueline's sake, Jack began paying more attention to what he wore. For the first time he began to appear publicly and regularly in suits that matched. The khaki slacks and sneakers went out the window—except for the really casual moments when they were appropriate. His male friends nodded their heads sadly and knowingly when they saw the transformation. In its own small way it was a sign that the country's leading ex-bachelor was on his way to being tamed. Women, of course, approved and gave Jacqueline a double A rating for the miracle she had wrought.

There was one area, though, where Jacqueline couldn't get him to meet her even halfway. He had absolutely no patience with her so-called "arty" friends. Whenever Jacqueline had them over the talk naturally drifted to things like literature, music and art. Such discussions bored Jack. He was a practical man who believed that to be worth anything an idea had to be useful. If it didn't have a goal that led to action and accomplishment, he wasn't interested. It would take time for Jacqueline to teach him that practicality wasn't everything, and that the world of culture had pleasures and rewards worth seeking.

The Senator could be trying in other ways, too. He had, for instance, a most unfortunate habit of suddenly showing up with visitors Jacqueline hadn't been expecting. It called for all of his wife's ingenuity when such emergency situations arose. One in particular made her shudder for years afterward when she thought about it. One morning Jack turned to her casually and said,

"What are you serving our guests for lunch?" This was the first Jacqueline knew that she would be playing hostess to forty people in exactly two hours. The forty were properly fed and entertained but only as the result of a superhuman effort on Jacqueline's part. She had one word to describe her reaction to Jack's announcement that morning: "Panic!"

Then there was life at Hyannis Port with the Kennedys. When they stayed at Hyannis Port they were expected to have dinner with Jack's parents every night. After a long stretch of this, Jacqueline rebelled. Once a week is enough, she pointed out firmly, and had her way. She was also getting tired of being a touch football player. She had neither the talent nor the desire to excel as a football star. That was strictly a Kennedy trait. The last straw was when she broke her ankle during a typically furious session. It marked her permanent retirement from pigskin competition.

All these incidents, part of the natural hazards of early married life, led to stresses and strains. The situation wasn't helped by Jack's bad back. As the pain in his back increased, so did Jack's irritability. They both found their nerves being frazzled and upset by little things. Even buying a home of their own near Merrywood—Hickory Hill—didn't help too much. The traffic driving home from Washington at day's end was impossibly heavy. Jack's temper was mighty short by the time he worked his way through the hordes of cars and drove across the bridge to Virginia.

He was worried about his back and how it might affect his career. He was unable to attend sessions of the Senate now without the use of crutches. Nevertheless, he dragged himself in dutifully, grimly concluding the business for which the people had elected him. "The last day of the session," said his secretary, Mrs. Evelyn Lincoln, "he was in tremendous pain."

One of his friends was amazed that he was even able to get about. "That metal plate they put into his spine after the war had never healed over," he said. "You could look into an open hole in his back and see it."

Jack Kennedy never spoke of his pain, and when the occasion demanded he ignored it. Few people who saw him make speeches to audiences in those days were aware of his suffering. Just before going on he would hand his crutches to an aide. Then, no matter how much it hurt, he would pull himself together. Shoulders squared, chin erect, he would stride out across the platform flashing that famous grin as if he hadn't a care in the world. It was a good act and it fooled almost everyone.

The only one he wasn't fooling about his condition was himself—and Jacqueline. They both knew judgment day was coming and dreaded the moment when they would have to face it. Jacqueline wanted to help but she didn't know where to begin or how. They were two spirited, sensitive, intelligent, proud, strong-willed people who loved and needed each other and yet found themselves pulling in opposite directions. It would take several crises in their lives before they found their way to mutual love and understanding.

They suffered their first sorrow together almost a year after their marriage when Jacqueline, who had been pregnant, lost the child by miscarriage. It was a moment of grief for them both, for more than anything they wanted children. In the midst of his pain, Jack found words of solace for his wife.

A month later they faced their first real crisis. Jack had come to a decision about his back. The pain had become excruciating. He could no longer walk without crutches. Doctors told him that without an operation he would have to use them all the time. The prospect dismayed him. "I'd rather die than spend the rest of my life on these things," he said grimly.

"That was the only time he ever mentioned pain to me," said an old political friend, Frank Morrissey. "He told me he'd take the chance of dying—he couldn't stand any more pain."

There was fear in Jacqueline's heart as Jack set off for Manhattan's Hospital for General Surgery in New York.

But she put a brave smile on her face and went with him. She and Jack both knew that he might not survive. Aside from the danger of the surgery itself, there were other complicating factors.

Jack suffered from a condition known as *adrenal insufficiency*. It had been brought about by his wartime experiences and illnesses. By itself the condition was not serious. But under the stress of major surgery it might tip the scales of life and death one way or the other. It was this knowledge that both Jack and Jacqueline carried with them when he entered the hospital on October 21, 1954.

The operation, a delicate fusion of spinal discs, lasted for hours. When it was over Kennedy's life began to flicker on and off, like a candle in the wind. A priest was called in to say the last rites. Jacqueline and the rest of the Kennedys stood outside his door and prayed for his life. Their prayers were answered. He pulled back from the shadows and rallied.

Several months later, in February, 1955, it was necessary to perform a second operation. Again the Senator almost died; again he recovered. The doctors called it a miracle and attributed it, at least in part, to his fierce will to live. In all this time, as he alternated between pain and death, Jacqueline was at his side constantly.

All the things he could not do for himself she helped

him do. It was even difficult for him, lying immobile, to read, so she read to him from his favorite books on government and politics. She brought him faith and hope and good cheer, and finally, when he could sit up, she arranged little amusements to brighten his days. Once she surprised him with balloons and a pop gun. He spent the rest of the day happily blasting these floating targets out of the air. Another time she played a trick on him that really made his eyes pop. The night nurses on duty were not the prettiest in the world. One night there was a knock at the door. Expecting the usual plain creature in cap and gown, Jack called, "Come in." He was hardly prepared for the shining vision of loveliness in nurse's costume who walked in. After he'd caught his breath he recognized actress Grace Kelly. She and Jacqueline— they had met earlier in the evening at a dinner party— had cooked up the scheme together. When Jacqueline poked her head in through the door with an impish look on her face, Jack was howling with laughter. It was reward enough. She was always busy thinking up new ways to tide him through another day, to see that his spirits didn't flag or his hopes dim.

At the end of the month he was able to walk out of the hospital under his own power. Then he was flown to Florida, to another hospital bed, and to lie out in the sun and recuperate. Most men would have been content to lie there with their pain and wait for nature to heal them. Not Jack Kennedy. Enforced idleness was his sworn enemy. The Kennedy blood cried out for action. He had to find an outlet for his restless mind and energy even in a hospital bed.

One day he found the answer—he would write a book. Letters from well-wishers had been coming in by the hundreds. One was from a ninety-year-old lady who'd been bedridden for years in her home in Cape Cod. She wrote: "Never voted for a Democrat in my life, Mr. Kennedy. But I want to vote for at least one before I die—might stand me in good stead up above. So I want you to be up to running in 1958. Don't waste away feeling sorry for yourself, young man. Keep busy. Do all the things you've never had time to do!"

Keep busy—do all the things you've never had time to do! The words stuck in his mind. They were also a call to action. For years he had been toying with the idea of writing another book but there had never been enough time. Now he had nothing but time.

He also knew the book he wanted to write. Its theme was courage—courage of a special kind. Political courage had its own rules and its own limits. As a professional politician, Kennedy knew how difficult it was to stand up for principle when the majority was against you. It was doubly difficult when sticking to your guns might mean political defeat and disgrace.

There were men in American life who had shown this kind of courage. They had stood up for the right as they saw it, come hell or high water. Some of their names were familiar to every American—John Quincy Adams, Daniel Webster. Others were not so familiar—Edmund Ross, Lucius Quintus Cincinnatus Lamar. All had been congressional lawmakers in the service of the American people and their own consciences. Kennedy wanted to tell their stories. He even had a title for the book—*Profiles in Courage.*

The writing of the book was tackled in the same way he did everything—with zest and joy and total commitment. He gave it the full measure of his time and mind. He needed help. There were books and documents to be gotten from libraries, facts to be tracked down. Helpless in bed, he had to call on others to lend a hand. His brilliant aide, Theodore Sorenson was a key figure in the shaping, sifting, thinking and planning that slowly brought the book into being. Historian friends read and criticized chapters as they were written. But above all there was Jacqueline, tireless in her love and warmth, who acted as his chief of staff in charge of field operations. With skill and intelligence she guided all research activities and funneled them to the sick bed that had become an efficient office. She helped him read material and organize it, and her criticisms of style and content were invaluable in the actual writing.

As the book progressed, so did the Senator. It had become an anodyne to his spirit, a reason for being. It put him back in touch with life and himself, and with the woman he had married. It might easily have occurred to someone at the time that, by his own example, in the writing of this book, Jack Kennedy was himself a profile in courage.

At last it was finished. The mountain of labor and research had been boiled down into a tidy manuscript that was sent off to the fine old publishing house of Harper and Brothers which had agreed to publish the book. *Profiles in Courage* came out early in 1956 and scored an immediate success. Reviewers praised it as popular history at its best. Even professional historians liked it. They were impressed by its solid research and genuine literary distinction. Many people were surprised to see Kennedy write such a work. They hadn't ever thought of him as a man of letters. They forgot that he'd written his first book—*Why England Slept*—at the tender age of twenty-three. Even that youthful effort, though written by an unknown, had been a Book-of-the-Month Club selection and had sold eighty thousand copies.

Jacqueline was proud of the book and prouder still of Jack for having written it. She had a double stake in it, for much of her had gone into its making. Only Jack really knew how much. He dedicated the book to her and, in the preface he wrote, he told of the vital part she had played. To Jacqueline, however, there was something even more important. Jack had survived his ordeal. He had made a gallant stand against death and fought his way back. Then, in his crucible of pain, he had found a reason for living and doing in a book. So it was more than a mere book he had written. It was an answer he had given to the most severe challenge of body and mind he had ever faced.

His back would never be completely healed, but at least he could walk all by himself. In the spring of 1955, when he had returned to Washington, he looked tanned and fit. He had been gone seven long months. When reporters interviewed him they asked him where his crutches were. "I threw them away two days ago," he said, smiling. And he had.

Just to show them how well he was, he climbed the steps leading to the Capitol, then took Jacqueline for a stroll through the Capitol park. There was a slight, scarcely noticeable limp. Outside of that he seemed brimming with health and in the pink of condition.

On May 24, 1955 he had walked into the Senate for the

first time after his lengthy absence. Every senator rose to his feet and applauded. "We're glad to see you back, Jack," said the Democratic leader, Lyndon Johnson. They were, indeed.

Jack Kennedy had returned to the political wars.

Years of Storm and Lightning

The sight of Jack Kennedy in full sail again was a sight to behold. He was like a hurricane that had been held in check for too long and then unleashed. There was work to be done. His desk at the Senate was piled high with problems waiting to be solved. He waded into them with characteristic vim. His energy was boundless. He set a furious pace that left his staff limp and dragging.

A vivid picture of him in action was given by Jacqueline, who told a reporter, "I married a whirlwind . . . People who try to keep up with him drop like flies, including me."

The question was—where was this whirlwind heading and what would he reap?

Jacqueline was still not wild about politics, but she had gotten easier about it. If she had learned anything during Jack's drawn-out illness, it was patience. She had also gotten a closeup look at courage in the face of adversity and pain. The test had been mainly Jack's, but it had also been hers. She had come through her part of it with flying colors. Jack had summed up her behavior in two admiring words, "She's terrific!"

They had both profited from the experience. Jack was a little quieter than he had been. There was a firmer jut to his jaw and a harder glint in his gray eyes. But he was kinder and more considerate. Jacqueline, too, had grown more tender. Something had been stirred in her by Jack's helplessness and need. She had responded and become more of a woman, surer of herself and of him.

They went back to live in their house in Virginia—Hickory Hill. On its huge grounds were stables, an orchard, a swimming pool. The house itself was large with too many rooms for just two people. There was also a nursery that they both hoped would be filled soon.

Jacqueline loved the surrounding countryside with all its memories of her young girlhood. Many a day she mounted a horse and rode down familiar winding trails and across open fields where she could break into a gallop and feel the rushing wind. And sometimes, on mornings bright with spring or smoky with the light of autumn, she took an easel and paints outdoors and found a spot she liked. It really didn't matter if the picture came out just right. It was always so hard to catch on the wing the blending colors and shifting patterns of light. But it was fun to try.

During his illness she had even gotten Jack to paint. He had been reluctant at first. Then he had tried it and you couldn't get him to stop. Some of his landscapes were very good, too. Many people who saw them thought he had a first-rate talent. But now there was no time for anything so frivolous. He was far too busy, with too many other things on his mind. She could almost sense something brewing.

For Jacqueline had learned something else living with Jack—that you could always expect something new from him. His restless, probing mind was always seeking fresh challenges and greener fields to conquer. Like the warriors of old, he was geared for combat. What would it be this time?

It didn't take her long to find out. Jack Kennedy had

just survived one ordeal; he was now ready for another. This time, though, his goal was an audacious one, beyond anything he had yet attempted. He had decided to seek the Presidency of the United States.

Certainly, the very idea was enough to take your breath away. Many men had sought this office. Most had failed. But that didn't deter Jack, even though he had two strikes on him before he started. For one thing, he was much too young. There was a tradition in American life which said that a man had to grow old and wise in the service of his country before he was allowed to try for the Presidency. Even more important was Jack's religion. He was a Catholic. So far no Catholic had ever been elected to either of the two top offices in the country. Al Smith, who had tried in 1928 when he opposed Herbert Hoover for the Presidency, had been roundly and sadly trounced in a campaign notorious for its bigotry.

These were but two of the obstacles Jack had to hurdle in his quest for the golden prize. He still had to get the politicians in his own party to accept him and to nominate him. Then he had to convince the voters that he was the right man and get them to elect him. It would take a lot of doing.

His campaign began in the spring of 1956 when he was not quite thirty-nine years old. He did not launch it full-blown and aim for the top spot at one stroke. He would have to move slowly, one step at a time.

First he would try for the Vice-Presidency. The National Convention of the Democratic party would be meeting in the summer. The delegates to the convention would at that time select two men to head the party's national ticket in the November elections. Adlai Stevenson of Illinois was almost certain to be the Presidential nominee for the second time in a row. Jack wanted to be his Vice-Presidential running mate.

He and his chief of staff, Ted Sorenson, went to work trying to round up support for Jack. So did the other members of the Kennedy family. Father Joe Kennedy stayed in the background but he was busy on the telephone calling influential people he knew. The Kennedy camp also circulated a private report which showed that one of the reasons Stevenson had been beaten by Eisenhower in 1952 was because he had lost the Catholic vote. Jack was a Catholic—and popular. The top brass in the Democratic party could draw their own conclusions.

By the time the convention had rolled around, in mid-August, Jack was one of the leading contenders for the Vice-Presidency. There were also many other outstanding aspirants, among them Hubert Humphrey and Estes Kefauver. Stevenson, however, was playing it cool. He had as yet given no real hint of his choice.

Chicago was blazing hot that time of year. A searing wind blew and kept blowing in from the prairies. In a famous poem once, Carl Sandburg had called the windy city "hog butcher of the world," and this time of the year it smelled it. The delegates—more than a thousand of them—thanked God for their air-conditioned hotel rooms. Into this modern setting of Dante's *Inferno* came Jack and Jacqueline Kennedy to see what fortune would bring their way. Jacqueline was pregnant again, in her sixth month, and not feeling very well. But she had come because Jack might get the nomination and she wanted to be there if he did.

Jack set up headquarters at the Conrad Hilton Hotel and sent his ailing wife to stay with his sister, Eunice Shriver, who lived in Chicago. He wanted to keep her away from the hustle and bustle of the politicking that would be going on in his suite. She could watch the convention on television. But there was too much excitement in the air for her to stay away. When Jack was picked to make the nominating speech for Stevenson she just had to be there to see it and hear it. So she sat in a box set aside for her and looked down at the proceedings on the convention floor—first a prayer, then the playing of *The Star Spangled Banner,* and then chairman Sam Rayburn of Texas bringing the delegates to order.

Then it was Jack's turn and she held her breath, listening to the familiar tones ring out, so familiar to her and yet suddenly strange and remote inside the glare of the spotlight that shone down on him. It was a good speech, full of fine-sounding phrases. He and his staff had worked on it all night after the Stevenson people gave them the word that Jack was to make it. Now here it was, all polished, words carefully chosen, nobody aware of all the times it had been rewritten and agonized over.

Somewhere down on the floor was Ted Sorenson, Jack's good right arm, and his brother Bob who was becoming a big factor in the Kennedy organization. Bobby was the Kennedy said to be the one most like his father, which made him disliked by many people who disliked his father. But Jacqueline liked Bobby a lot, the best, as a matter of fact, of all the Kennedys; the one for whom, as she was to say, she would "put her arm in the fire for." Things had gotten a lot easier for Jacqueline with the Kennedys. She had once thought they would dislike her for all the ways in which she was different from them. But she had found out that it was just the opposite—that they liked her *because* she was different and were proud of her. There was just no predicting that unpredictable clan.

After Jack's speech and Stevenson's nomination, which went as planned, there was lots of huddling in the hotel rooms. Nobody knew who Stevenson would pick as his running mate. All the hopefuls bit their fingernails and waited. Then came the dramatic announcement. Stevenson had thrown the nomination open to the convention.

It would be the delegates, not he, who would do the choosing. The Stevenson bombshell left everyone stunned. But not for long. There began a mad, frenzied scramble for delegate votes. It was as if all the waters of the dams had broken loose.

All night long the hunt for votes went on. By morning, when the convention opened, it was still going on. Down on the floor Bob Kennedy was hustling around trying to pick up votes for his brother, wheedling, cajoling, threatening, as the case demanded. Other lieutenants of other camps were doing the same. Jack Kennedy had moved his command post to rooms at the Stockyard Inn because it was close to the International Amphitheatre, site of the convention. From there he directed operations, kept in touch with his floor leaders, and watched the drama unfold on television.

Jacqueline was at the convention itself. She had found it impossible to sit tight at sister-in-law Eunice's while Jack was in the most important fight of his political life. So she had dragged herself down through the oppressive heat and into the roaring heart of the convention where Jack's fate would soon be decided.

Well-wishers came to crowd around her in her box, to tell her how much they wanted Jack to win and how hard they were rooting for him. She didn't even know many of the people but she kept nodding her head and smiling and saying, "Thank you" in that politely modulated voice that had been trained in the best schools.

Then the balloting began, state by state, the chairman of each delegation rising to announce how the votes in his state were being cast. When the first ballot had been completed, Senator Estes Kefauver was leading. Jack was second. Then came two other Senators in third and fourth place, Albert Gore and Hubert Humphrey. On the second ballot Gore and Humphrey dropped out of contention. Now Jack began to pick up strength. When the state of Texas was polled, its chairman, Lyndon Johnson, rose to cast all its fifty-six votes for "the fighting young sailor who bears the scars of battle, Jack Kennedy." An uproar followed Johnson's declaration. Nothing, it now seemed, could stand in the way of Kennedy's nomination.

Jacqueline sat holding her breath, heart beating like a trip-hammer. Could it really be that Jack would win? But it wasn't to be—yet. At the end of the second ballot Jack was just short of victory. The third ballot should do it for sure.

As the third ballot began the Kennedy camp was getting all set to slap itself on the back. Their man now needed only thirty-eight and a half votes more to win and the bandwagon was rolling his way. One more key state and it would be all over. Back at the Stockyard Inn, Ted

Sorenson offered Jack his congratulations. Jack spurned the handshake. "Not yet," he said.

How right he was. No sooner had Sorenson spoken than the sentiment of the convention shifted. Two states switched their votes to Kefauver. Then another. Bedlam broke loose as other states began to follow suit. The thirty some odd votes which Jack needed for victory never came. The Kennedy bubble had burst. Kefauver had won.

In his room at the Inn, Jack gave Sorenson a grim, fatalistic grin and said, "Let's go." They departed for the convention.

In her box Jacqueline sat dazed. It had all happened too swiftly. Just minutes ago people had been thronging about her full of congratulations. Now she was all alone, deserted as if by magic. Now it was Nancy Kefauver, the winning candidate's wife, who was being mobbed in her box. Tears welled up in Jacqueline's eyes.

There was a commotion on the convention floor. She looked down, trying to see through the tears. It was Jack! There he stood on the platform, smiling and waving to the crowd. His voice drifted up to her as through a dream.

Gallant in defeat, gracious as ever, he moved that the nomination go to Kefauver unanimously. The convention rose to its feet and gave him a standing ovation.

Then Jack left the platform and disappeared inside a circle of backslappers and handshakers.

When the din had quieted, Jacqueline rose to leave. People opened a path for her, muttering words of sympathy as she went by. Somehow, among that milling throng, Jack found his way to her side. With him was an old friend, Senator George Smathers of Florida. The three left the convention together. The late afternoon sun outside was still blinding, the heat wet and soggy as a Turkish bath. Hardly a word was spoken during the cab ride back to Jack's hotel.

It wasn't much better in the hotel room. The loser's grin which Jack had flashed at millions of TV viewers around the country was gone now. His mood was one of deep, dark despair. He wasn't used to losing. He didn't like it.

One of the first things he did was make a phone call to his father who was summering on the French Riviera. He tried to take the edge of bitterness from his voice. "We did our best," he told Joe Kennedy. "I had fun and I didn't make a fool of myself."

He had, as a matter of fact, put up a showing that had electrified the whole country. He didn't know it then, but in defeat Jack Kennedy had won a victory of tremendous proportions. The American people had seen him in action and they liked what they had seen. They would not forget his good sportsmanship and his straight-forward manner. If ever a loser came out of a convention a winner it was Jack Kennedy. But he didn't know it then.

All he knew as he sat in that hotel room was that he had been beaten. Joe Kennedy had always taught his children that coming in second best doesn't count, that the only one people remember is the winner. In this contest Jack had emerged second best. He sat and brooded.

George Smathers, who sat there with Jack and Jacqueline for almost two hours, gave a graphic description of the atmosphere that prevailed in the room. "I've never been to an Irish wake before," said Smathers. "The three of us just sat around the hotel room, glum, none of us saying very much . . . He was hurt, deeply hurt. The thing is, he came so close."

Too close, and the wound was still too fresh for him to bear the pain by himself. Before the convention he had made plans to leave afterwards for a vacation on the Riviera with his father. He wanted that vacation more than ever now.

Perhaps he was too wrapped up in his own feelings to notice how deeply Jacqueline had been affected by his defeat. She couldn't bear to see him so unhappy. At that moment she wanted him to reach out for her and need her as she needed him. But he didn't. He flew off as planned to the Riviera. There was nothing for Jacqueline to do but take herself and her melancholy to her mother's summer place in Newport. It had been a grueling ordeal for her to undergo in her condition.

Jack probably never realized how much his wife needed him at that moment. He, too, was emotionally drained and sought to revive his spirits in the sun, sand and sea of the Mediterranean. He had long conversations with his father, then went off on a cruise with his brother Teddy. The sea had always been one of the places he loved best. It had a freshness and purity about it that made everything else seem old and tired. They swam and fished and let themselves go with the tide. Finally they put into port. A cablegram was waiting for Jack. It had grim news. Jacqueline had been rushed to the hospital. The baby, premature, had been stillborn. The doctors had performed surgery on Jacqueline. Her life was in grave danger.

There was no time for Jack to waste berating himself. When he reached the hospital in Newport Jacqueline was still very sick. But she was out of danger. What was there for him to say?

It was the low point of their marrriage. When Jacqueline left the hospital she could not bring herself to return to Hickory Hill, with its empty nursery and silent rooms.

The shadow of this sad event hung over their lives as they sought to find a way back to each other.

The next few months were hard ones for them to get through. They moved into an apartment in Washington. Hickory Hill was sold to Bob and Ethel Kennedy who filled it easily with their huge brood of children and an odd assortment of pets which included a show-off seal named Sandy.

Jack tried to make up to Jacqueline in little ways. He even gave French cooking a try. Still the rumors in the gossip columns would not let up. "The Kennedys were on the outs." "The Kennedys were breaking up." "It was only a matter of time before. . . ."

All such talk was put to rest in the spring of 1957 when word got out that Mrs. Kennedy was expecting another child in the fall. Then, in May, there came more good news when *Profiles in Courage* was awarded a Pulitzer prize for biography. It was an unexpected and overwhelming honor. As a result, Jack's political stock rose even higher.

He himself had bounced back from his low mood of the summer before. Summing it all up now, he realized that what had happened had actually worked out in his favor. Stevenson and Kefauver had been whipped by Eisenhower and Nixon in the fall campaign. Had he been on the ticket with Stevenson he might be a political has-been now. Instead he was more popular than ever. When a friend, reading the signs of the times, said to him, "You're certain to get the Vice-Presidential nomination in 1960," Jack grinned and replied, "I'm not running for Vice-President next time. I'm running for President."

And he was. His campaign for 1960 started early. Offers for him to make speeches came pouring in from all over the country. He was hard-pressed to fit them all into his itinerary.

The growing Kennedy popularity was a magical thing. Noting it, his father said proudly to a magazine interviewer, ". . . when his picture is on the cover of *Life* or *Redbook* . . . they . . . sell a record number of copies."

His magnetic personality and good looks didn't hurt, either. James Reston of the New York *Times* wrote that "the effect he has on women voters is almost naughty."

Reston also pointed out another aspect of his appeal: the sober, scholarly side of the young man from Massachusetts. His speeches, reported Reston, were filled with "learned quotations from Shakespeare, Justice Holmes, Woodrow Wilson, and the Founding Fathers." Voters found him ". . . serious and personable . . . with a fresh personality."

The same judgment about him was being rendered wherever his speaking trips took him—in every state of the union.

Jacqueline did little traveling with him now. They both wanted to make sure that nothing went wrong this time. As summer waned and autumn came to Washington, the Kennedys began making preparations for the baby's arrival. On the day after Thanksgiving Jacqueline gave birth to a golden-haired girl. It was a red-letter day for both her and Jack. They named the child Caroline.

The birth of a baby in any household is always a happy and joyous occasion. For Jacqueline and her husband it was a twice-blessed event. They had endured much to reach this moment. They could only marvel and wonder at the beautiful child lying in her crib who had come into their lives and home and made them one. Now they were a family. There were many nights when Jacqueline fought sleep, wanting to stay awake so she could think some more about the miracle of it; or to get up softly in the dark and take one more look at the child who had made her a mother.

Jack Kennedy, too, had waited eagerly for fatherhood. The Kennedys were a family full of children. He had nieces and nephews galore whom he loved dearly. But to have one's own—that was the miracle of life. Jacqueline saw his happiness and was glad as a mother always is when her child is loved by the man she loves. The sadness of the year before, when she had lost her second child, was washed away. Now she and Jack were truly together and their marriage had a meaning it had never had before.

There was a need for a house of their own now, and Jacqueline had found the perfect one in Georgetown. It was made of red brick and Jacqueline fell in love with it as soon as she saw it. When Caroline was three weeks old they moved in. Soon Jacqueline had put her own stamp on it. The French touch was everywhere—Louis XVI chairs in the dining room, French porcelain on the shelves, and even a French clock on the mantel. The walls were hung with pictures they loved, the bookcases filled with their favorite books. It was of this house that Jacqueline said, "I love our home in Washington. There has always been a child in it . . . My sweet little house leans slightly to one side, and the stairs creak."

As Caroline grew, both parents took pride in each landmark of her growth—the first tooth, the first word, the first toddling steps. Jacqueline was amused at how the man who would be President fell prey to a little girl's wiles, touched by his gentleness and kindness with her. "He is so affectionate with his daughter," said Jacqueline about her husband. "She has made him so much happier. A man without a child is incomplete."

The house on N Street in Georgetown—the little house that leaned—was the best and happiest place they had lived in. They had people in to dinner and sat around the fire afterwards talking the night away. Many of them were old friends—Charlie Bartlett and his wife, the Benjamin Bradlees, Rowland Evans and his wife. It was surprising how many of the people they liked were journalists. Bartlett was the Washington correspondent of the Chattanooga *Times,* Ben Bradlee was on the staff of *Newsweek,* and Rowland Evans wrote a syndicated column for the New York *Herald Tribune.*

There were other things to be thankful for. Jack no longer found his wife's friends so hard to take. One of them got along especially well with Jack. This was William Walton, the painter. He was particularly welcome because he could switch the conversation from art with Jacqueline to politics with Jack and be equally at home in both. A rare friend, indeed. Jack even accompanied his wife occasionally to a museum or an art gallery, and a concert or two.

But he was still busy as ever—lunches on the run—never enough sleep. At the office he might go through an entire day on just a sandwich or a bar of chocolate. Jacqueline finally put a stop to that. She sent hot lunches over to his office in a covered hot plate—the same kind mothers use for feeding infants. Then Jack had to sit still long enough to get a good meal down. Several other Senators got wind of Kennedy's lunches and put in an order for the same. Soon three or four hot plates were being sent out daily to the Senate building from the house on N Street.

In 1958 Jack was faced with the problem of getting reelected to the Senate. Jacqueline, who had never taken too much part in his previous campaigns, went with him on this one. She traveled all up and down the state with her husband, adding her charm and glamor to his. Together, their good looks made a double visual impact on their audiences. The results were to show up on election night.

Jacqueline also got a good look at Massachusetts, which they covered from one end to another. Jack wanted to pile up a big majority and he wasn't ignoring a single voter. Once they even stopped off at a convent so he could talk to the nuns. He hadn't forgotten that nuns vote, too.

Historic Massachusetts made an impression on Jacqueline. "I'm so glad Jack comes from Massachusetts," she said, "because it's the state with the most history. Driving from one rally to another, we'd pass John Quincy Adams' house or Harvard—or Plymouth. I think I know every corner of Massachusetts."

And Massachusetts got to know her—and like her. Jacqueline was upper class but she never played down or up to the crowd. That kind of thing she left to the politicians. She did all right just by being herself and added a new element to the Kennedy campaigning style. The election totals proved it. Jack won by a whopping plurality of 874,608 votes—the largest margin of victory in the state's history.

His tremendous win in his home state gave Jack a big boost in the Presidential sweepstakes. He would be a hard man to overlook when it came time to choose a Presidential candidate in 1960. Jack wasn't going to give them a chance to overlook him. Right after the Massachusetts campaign he began his pursuit of the Presidency in earnest. The polls began to show that among all the potential contenders for the nomination he was the front-runner.

Some members of his staff were worried because they thought he was making his move too early. Front-runners, they knew from past political experience, rarely lasted into the home stretch. But Jack had another theory. There was such a thing, he told them, as getting so far out in front that nobody could catch you. This was an idea that was destined to shake up American politics as it had never been shaken up before.

Nineteen fifty-nine was a year of hard, intensive work. More than ten thousand invitations came in for the Senator to make appearances and speeches. He had to pick and choose among them in the light of his overall strategy. Each one was carefully weighed and considered. The Kennedy camp didn't want to offend anybody.

Jack's big push on the political front was an all-out effort. It was bound to put an added strain on Jacqueline. He had always kept her in the rear lines of his political wars. Now it would be impossible to protect her completely. How would she react to all the publicity, the traveling and campaigning, the intrusion on her family life?

He needn't have worried. As her artist friend, William Walton, was to put it, underneath her fine breeding and patrician manner, Jacqueline was a "strong dame." She proved it during the next few years. As Jack went up and down the country seeking support, Jacqueline was often at his side. At the same time she tried not to neglect her home or her child. Being a wife and mother was still the most important thing to her.

Jack also had the help of the whole Kennedy family, something that always happened when he had a fight on his hands. When the Kennedys smelled battle they came running. They also contributed a huge Convair airliner that became the aerial workhorse of the Kennedy operation. It flew Jack and his staff from place to place in lightning sorties that were as precisely planned as military invasions.

Nineteen sixty loomed as the crucial year. Jack was heading for some important primary fights that would either make him or break him. He had to win every contest he entered. Just one loss and he was finished. That was the fate of front-runners. If they wanted to win they had to get out in front and stay there until convention time. And even then it wasn't certain.

Primaries are important parts of the process of selecting Presidential candidates. Both major parties hold separate primaries in different states. Presidential hopefuls from each party vie with each other in these runoffs. The winner in each state gets either all or a majority of the delegate votes which the state party commands at the national convention. Not all states hold primaries, but those that do have an important say about who is chosen as the candidate of each party. Thus, say, if New York were to have a primary (which it doesn't), the winner would take to the convention all or a major portion of its ninety-eight votes. Such a commanding bloc of votes could easily swing the nomination one way or another.

These were the prizes Jack was after as he began his hunt for delegate votes in 1960.

The first primary contest, in New Hampshire, was easy. Jack won handily there. But that was to be expected. He was a New Englander and he was fighting on home territory. The next two, however—Wisconsin and West Virginia—would be the decisive ones. These two tests of the Kennedy vote-getting ability would either make him or break him. The Kennedy forces girded their loins for combat.

Jacqueline joined the Kennedy troops as they invaded

Wisconsin. She wanted to be at her husband's side—even though she had just learned she was pregnant again. Doctors told her to take it easy. Her past history in these matters made it important that she didn't exhaust herself.

She was a big help to Jack in Wisconsin. She traveled all over the state with him by plane and by car. She made speeches and shook hands. She even found herself being caught up in the excitement of the struggle. After all these years she was actually beginning to enjoy campaigning.

The Wisconsin voters loved her. The women liked her clothes and her looks. The men were full of admiration for her spunk. It was an old pioneer tradition for women to keep on with the work even though they were with child. And here was Jacqueline, doing just that, stumping the state with her husband, lovely and fragile-looking, but deceptively tough.

Some of the Wisconsin farmers were indifferent to the candidate but not to his wife. One of them, asked what he thought about Kennedy, replied with a grin, "Well, he's got a beautiful wife."

On April 5, Wisconsin voters went to the polls. By evening the decision was in. Jack had won a victory—a narrow one—over Senator Hubert Humphrey of Minnesota. That was one hurdle out of the way. Next, and even more important, there would be West Virginia.

It was in this small state that Jack's religion became the

major issue of the campagin. Could a Catholic be trusted in the White House? To whom would he owe his prior allegiance—to the United States or to the Pope? The same kind of anti-Catholic sentiment that had beaten Al Smith in 1928 could now prove the downfall of John F. Kennedy in 1960.

Jack met the issue head-on. He went on television and explained his position. He stood for complete separation of church and state. He told the people of West Virginia—and the nation—that when a President takes his oath of office he swears on the Bible. For him to break that solemn oath would be not only a violation of his trust but a grievous sin against God. If he were President, his Presidential duties and loyalties would come first. This was the promise he made that day.

It was the most dramatic moment of the West Virginia campaign. More important, it convinced the voters of that state that he meant what he said. From that day forward the religious issue became secondary. The candidates would now be judged on their merits.

Jack won the West Virginia primary by a convincing margin. There was not a flicker of doubt in anyone's mind now. The front-runner was not only out in front now, he was pulling still further ahead.

The rest of the primaries were easy. One after another they fell like ripe plums into Jack's lap—Maryland, Oregon, Indiana, Nebraska. The Kennedy bandwagon was moving toward the convention under a full head of steam.

Jacqueline was spending most of her time at home now. Jack wanted her to stay with their child and conserve her strength. There would be an arduous campaign coming up in the fall, if and when he won the nomination. In 1956 she had attended the national convention in Chicago with Jack. She had been pregnant then, too. The memory of that occasion was still an unpleasant one. This time the convention would meet in Los Angeles, in July. As Jack departed for the West Coast, Jacqueline remained behind in the summer house they had bought in Hyannis Port.

The fight for the Presidential nomination at Los Angeles was no contest. Jack won in a walk. There were a few attempts made to stop him. They all failed.

The balloting began on the evening of July 14. Jacqueline spent that critical evening painting a picture. The television set was turned on in another room. In front of it sat her mother and stepfather who had come to share this momentous night with her. They kept flashing excited reports to Jacqueline. Between brushstrokes Jacqueline ran in to see for herself. She gazed at the set wide-eyed with wonder as Wyoming cast the ballots that put Jack over the top. Her husband had been nominated for

President of the United States. He had won on the very first ballot, just as he had planned. Not too long ago, when newspapermen had questioned her about Jack, she had told them she believed that he could do anything he set his mind to do. She believed that more than ever now. Drawing a deep breath she went back to the other room to work some more at her painting.

Not long after, the telephone rang. She picked it up, knowing at once that it could only be Jack. At his greatest moment of victory he had thought about Jacqueline. She tried to keep the tremble out of her voice. She was so happy for him!

Later, in the wee hours of the morning, she went out to talk to reporters who were clustered on the porch. Flash-bulbs popped. TV cameras pinpointed in on her. She didn't have much to say. What was there to say that had not already been said a thousand times? So many years had gone into the making of this night. Her words were simple. "He worked so hard," she said. It told the whole story.

When Jack came back to Hyannis Port after the convention, the painting was all finished. It was one of Jacqueline's most humorous, brimming over with her light, gay, lilting sense of fun. There was Jack in a boat which she had dubbed *Victura II,* after his own favorite sloop. Dressed in a Napoleonic costume, the conquering hero was surrounded by members of his family. A nearby ship fired saluting salvos from its guns. A plane roared overhead, trailing a sign that read: "You've done it again, Johnny . . ." On the dock, waiting to greet him, was Jacqueline, Caroline, her nurse, a dog, and a brass band. Lined up on the beach were more cheering people. At the sight of this gently ribbing portrait, bubbling with love and humor, the victorious candidate broke into a delighted grin of appreciation. It was a wonderful welcome-home present.

Now one last task remained—the election itself. The Republicans had nominated Richard Nixon for President and Henry Cabot Lodge for Vice-President. It was this duo which Jack and his running mate, Lyndon Johnson, would have to face in November. Both Nixon and Lodge were old friends—and old enemies. He had known Dick Nixon since back in the days when they were young congressmen together. It was Henry Cabot Lodge, from his own home state of Massachusetts, whom he had defeated when he ran for the Senate for the first time in 1952. They were both veteran campaigners who knew how to box and how to slug. Jack looked forward to a bruising battle.

Jacqueline could not do too much in the Presidential campaign. She was already well advanced in her pregnancy. The baby was due in December. But she did the best and the most that she could to help her husband become President. She made appearances on television and handled herself wittily and skillfully at press conferences. She also made some speeches, wrote hundreds of letters and turned out a weekly newspaper column called "Campaign Wife."

One of the most poignant moments in the campaign occurred for her during a mammoth ticker tape parade in New York City. She and Jack were riding in an open car that moved slowly along Wall Street, in the heart of the city's financial district. It was here, many years ago, that John Vernou Bouvier III had taken his daughter to see the mad doings on the floor of the New York Stock Exchange. Memories of that wonderful day came crowding through her mind now. Just then, Jack leaned over and said, "Isn't it too bad that your father couldn't be with us in this car today. He'd have really enjoyed seeing this." It was almost as if he had been reading her mind. Jacqueline nodded her head. Her eyes were misty and shining.

The sound and fury of the campaign continued until the very last day, leaving a trail of promises and oratory behind it. The candidates had traveled thousands of miles and made hundreds of speeches. They had crossed verbal swords in their famous television debates that had been watched by millions. Now only the echoes remained. Now the last act was about to be played. At this moment of the drama the candidates withdrew from the scene. It was time for the American people to take the center of the stage. In towns and villages, cities and hamlets, they would go to the ballot boxes. On this one day, and for one day only, they would speak as with one voice, and out of the judgment they rendered would come a man they deemed fit to be President of the United States. It was the wonder and glory of the thing men called democracy.

Election day, 1960, began bright and early for Jack Kennedy and his wife. They drove from their Boston hotel to an old, no longer used public library where they were to vote. When they arrived there was a crowd waiting. Newspaper reporters followed hard on their heels as they walked up the steps. Jack kept trying to protect Jacqueline, in her eighth month of pregnancy, from the press of people around them. After they had both voted —about fifteen minutes before nine—they left quickly and the procession of cars, of which their closed convertible was one, moved on to the airport. Twenty-five minutes after they had boarded the plane they were in Hyannis Port.

Jack had brought along something for Caroline—a huge bag of toys which he had collected on his campaign trips around the country. Her eyes really lit up when she saw it. They had breakfast at father Joe Kennedy's house with the rest of the family. Later, around noon, Jack went out and passed a football around with brothers Bob and Ted. After lunch he went to Bob's house to look over the equipment that had been installed there—direct wire telephones and teletype machines—for reports that would be coming in that evening from key points of the nation.

At mid-afternoon, around half-past three, Jack went back to his own place to try to nap. Richard Nixon was trying to do the same thing at about the same time in California. It would be a long night and a longer morning after that for both of them.

No election in recent memory was as close or as tense as this one. First, in the early hours of the evening, it was Jack Kennedy who took a big lead that seemed insurmountable. But slowly, as the night progressed, returns from the midwest and then the far west cut that lead to the point where everything was uncertain. When Jack Kennedy went to sleep at almost 4 A.M. there was still no winner. But when he awoke some time after nine that same morning, he was the same man he had been before except for one thing. He was now the President-elect of the United States.

Jack Kennedy had won. Richard Nixon had lost. By a paper-thin margin of 119,450 votes out of 68,836,385 that had been cast he had defeated his rival for the highest office in the land. This figure represented only one-tenth of one percent of the total vote but it might just as well have been one-hundred percent, for all that it mattered.

The momentous event brought instant change into the life of the new President. Members of the Secret Service arrived to throw up a protective screen around him. From now on they would be with him always, casting their shadows across his figure wherever he went.

On that same morning of his victory Jack Kennedy had looked about him and noticed that his wife was missing. "Where's Jackie?" he had asked. Someone had seen her out on the beach. She had gone out there, in an old raincoat, to walk and be by herself. We do not know what it was she thinking in those moments, but it could only have been about the extraordinary thing that had just happened to her and her husband. He was now the President. She was his First Lady. How would this affect all their lives—their daughter Caroline's and the new child who would be born next month? Soon they would all four of them be taking up residence in that awesome dwelling, the White House. Her mind, still tuned to the warmth and privacy of their home in Georgetown, could not yet grasp the enormity of the change, nor even begin to cope with it.

The President himself went out to get her. For a moment, they walked hand in hand along the beach, watching the waves come in and the gulls soaring, sweeping, sailing above them. It was a moment etched in time and loneliness for these two people who had suddenly become different and would now have to bear the unknown burdens and the uncertain glories together. Something old had ended. It would never be the same for them again.

At age forty-three John F. Kennedy was the youngest man ever elected to the American Presidency. At thirty-one his wife Jacqueline would be the third-youngest First Lady to enter the White House.

A new era in American life, bright with the promise of youth and fresh hope, was about to begin.

Years of Grace and Greatness

CHAPTER SEVEN

It snowed on the morning of Inauguration Day, January 20, 1961. Around nine o'clock the snow stopped. It grew bitingly cold, with a whipping wind and bright frosty sunlight. Shortly before noon the old President and the new President rode together to the Capitol where the new President would be sworn in. They walked up the Capitol steps, the old President going first, as was still the privilege of his office.

127

A note of expectancy hung in the air. What would the new President say? What note would he strike?

The ceremonies began dramatically. An old man stepped to the lectern—America's good gray poet, Robert Frost. He had been invited as a special guest to read one of his poems. The quavering voice began, then stopped. The sunlight was too bright, too blinding. He couldn't see the words on the paper he held. There was a stirring behind him. Someone—it was the new Vice-President—came forward to shield him from the sun. The voice went on, "The land was ours before we were the land's. . . ."

Already this was something new—the first time a poet had been part of an Inauguration ceremony. It was a tribute to all poets. Was this a portent of the kind of thing one could expect from the new President? A silence that had the hush of history on it fell as John F. Kennedy came forward to take his oath of office. Then he began his Inaugural Address.

He left no doubt that the keynote of his program was the word *new*. It already had a name—the New Frontier. "The torch has been passed to a new generation of Americans," he declared. His address rang with other challenging phrases. "Let us begin. . . ." he cried. ". . . Ask not what your country can do for you—ask what you can do for your country. . . ."

The new President's wife watched proudly. She wore a

plain cloth coat against the cold. It stood out strangely in the sea of furs worn by the other ladies who were present. After he had taken the applause of the crowd, the new President smiled at his wife and winked. She winked back, smiling too.

They rode back through the Washington streets packed tight with cheering people. It would be like this always now, cheers, applause, waving of hands. The new President and his new First Lady waved back. There would be much celebrating throughout the day, followed by a gala Inaugural Ball in the evening. In the meanwhile, they went home.

"Home" was now the White House. It was a strange word to use about that austere, forbidding place. It was more like a museum or a monument, but one would hardly call it a home. Yet this was now where they would be living, for four or perhaps eight years. And here it was that they would be raising their children—for there were now two, four-year-old Caroline and not quite two-month-old John, Jr.

The new baby had been born to Jacqueline in late November, three weeks after her husband had been elected President. He had arrived suddenly, a month before he was expected. Quick action on the part of the doctor had saved his life. Now he was an active infant whose vigorous kicking and lusty cries made it hard to tell that he had been born prematurely.

Part of the fourteen-room Presidential apartment had been turned into a nursery. It looked strange there, to say the least. It would be stranger still to hear the baby's wails there in the dead of night and Caroline's shouts and laughter in the daytime.

It had been a wrench for Jacqueline to give up the little house on N Street. They had been so comfortable and so easy within its friendly walls. Despite all the politics and publicity when Jack had been a Senator it had still been a haven of privacy for them. Now, in this great big barn of a place, so formal and so formidable, it would be like living inside a goldfish bowl.

On their first night in the historic old mansion Jacqueline found all the windows sealed. She had them opened. Also, the fireplaces, of which there were many, hadn't been used in years. When they tried lighting fires in some of them the rooms filled up with soot and smoke. Everything was enormous. The shades worked on ropes and pulleys and were big enough to be ship's sails. The whole place had a shut-in feeling as if it were a world unto itself. When she looked outside she felt, as she told someone later, "like a moth banging on a windowpane."

The moth may have felt shut in but the world outside had its eye on her. There were always people at the fence which ran around the White House who did nothing but stand there and stare at the building. It was a real shock to her the first time she glanced down from her bedroom window and saw the faces pressed up against the iron bars looking, it seemed, straight at her. At Jack's inaugural she had been heard to say, "I feel as though I have just become a piece of public property." Now she understood the real meaning of that statement. It was the White House—perhaps the Presidency itself—that was the public's property. An accident of history had brought her there to live at the very center of national attention. Enduring the endless stares, the awe and the curiosity was the lot of all whose fate brought them to that house. Just a portion of it was set aside for the personal use of the President and his family. It was within this small enclave inside a national shrine that they were expected to carry on the intimate, human side of their affairs.

The President's living quarters are in a separate wing of the building. This is a part of the house tourists never see. Even a President has to have some privacy. On the second floor of the White House, the Presidential apartment is serviced by a concealed elevator which allows its occupants to come and go in private. Its last tenants, the Eisenhowers, had furnished it to their own tastes. Jacqueline now did it over in her own style. Soon her favorite pieces were gracing its rooms and halls. The paintings

and prints she loved were put on the walls. Jack's books
and hers went into the bookshelves. The children's rooms
were made bright and gay with color.

It took a while to get her bearings. There was so much
to do and so much to learn. Every day she found out
something new that had to be done by the First Lady. It
took up so much of her time that she had little left over
for the children. Every time she looked at Caroline she
saw a woeful little face staring back at her. It made her
heartsick to think she was neglecting her.

But it all straightened out in time. At the end of three
months she had it all in hand and running smoothly. She
had a right to feel proud of herself. She was also ex-
hausted.

Jack was getting the hang of his job, too. He was still
chipper and full of bounce. Sometimes she looked at him
and wondered where he got all his energy. He was working harder than ever. If he'd ever had the idea that the
Presidency would be a rest for him he had dropped that
notion quickly. Every night, at the end of his official day,
he came back up to the apartment with a folder full of
documents. Later, after dinner sometime, she'd hear the
rustle of papers from another room as he did his homework. There was always lots and lots of homework. He
had a tremendous capacity for work and never seemed to
mind doing it. His mind—like swift, darting quicksilver

—was never at rest even when he seemed to be relaxing. When she saw his gray eyes grow quizzical and start to stray she could almost see the machinery at work inside his head.

It was a remarkable thing about Jack how he kept growing all the time. His mind was marvelously open and receptive to everything. Something about him was always the perpetual student, wanting to learn, curious about another point of view because it might tell him something new. That was why he had always gotten smart people to work for him, why they liked working for him, too. He wasn't afraid of another man's brains. They were a challenge to his own, a counterforce against which to test his ideas and his thinking. All kinds of people—writers, educators, scientists, economists—were impressed by this mind that never stood still, that was always reaching out for more. His wife was, too. Once she said that if she were to draw a picture of him it would be that of a man with a very small body and an enormous head. It was a vivid and striking image.

It had been strange, at first, thinking about him as the "President." Others, too, who had been on friendly terms with him before the election had the same trouble, including members of his family. She remembered the day after election, for instance, at Hyannis Port. All the Kennedys had been out on the lawn playing touch football.

The President-elect, one of the players, had been trying his darndest to beat the opposition team headed by his brother Bobby. On one play the new President had leaped futilely for a pass and missed. "All guts and no brains," Bobby had observed. Even as he had said it everyone there had realized that this would be one of the last times he would be talking to his brother like that, that any of them, as a matter of fact, would be taking such liberties. From now on he would be "Mr. President."

It wasn't the man, it was the office. Something happened to a man when he became President. He became the office itself, an institution, the very embodiment of the government of the United States. People snapped to attention now when he walked by, became alert and listening when he spoke. The President, too, was aware of what had happened to him. When old friends called at the office they no longer boomed out, "Hi, Jack." It was now a discreet and respectful, "Hello, Mr. President." For a while, at the beginning of his term, he had tried to keep up the pretense that nothing had really changed. It was lonely up there at the peak of his eminence. But gradually, sadly, he realized that it was not to be, that he must accept himself just as others were accepting him. He must be "the President" even to himself.

The Presidency also brought about a change in John Kennedy's manners, or so it appeared to the naked eye.

When he is in the company of other people and there is a door to be gone through, custom demands that the President always go first. This even holds true when he is with his wife. Some people who saw him precede Jacqueline in such situations thought he was being rude and sent letters to that effect. It was not rudeness on the President's part. This is the respect due him by virtue of his office and even his wife must bow to this severe rule. Of course, when he was away from Washington, in the privacy of his own home, the President could go back to being a gentleman like any other man in the presence of a lady.

Told of the criticism that had been aroused by his seeming lack of courtesy toward his wife, the President said, with a twinkle in his eye, that "Jackie will just have to walk faster."

Shortly after he became chief executive, John Kennedy was visited by Eleanor Roosevelt, herself the wife of a President—Franklin D. Roosevelt. As they moved toward another room, the President held the door open for Mrs. Roosevelt.

"No," said the former First Lady. "You go first. You are the President."

"I keep forgetting," he said with a laugh.

"You must never forget," said Mrs. Roosevelt softly. And she meant it; it just wasn't allowed.

Some of the majesty of her husband's office had already rubbed off on Jacqueline. There was nothing official about her role of First Lady. She was just the wife of the President. And yet the wife of the President was not just a wife like other wives. She didn't just preside over a household. She was really a first mate aboard the Ship of State. As such, she had some solemn duties to perform even though they weren't spelled out in a formal way.

There were, to begin with, all the official receptions and state dinners. As First Lady, Jacqueline had to act as hostess. Other First Ladies had left the planning of these affairs to the White House staff. But Jacqueline felt it her responsibility to supervise them herself. She worked out the menus with the chefs, took care of the seating arrangements, and even chose the flowers for the table.

She had gotten to meet a lot of interesting people on these occasions. The great and notable of the world beat a steady path to the White House door. One week it might be Prime Minister Macmillan of Britain, the next, Nehru of India. Preparing for these ceremonials, let alone just getting through them, was hard work. Every time a foreign statesman came to call, Jacqueline had to be briefed on both him and his country so that she would know what to talk about. Jack, of course, had absolutely no trouble. He already knew everything.

Visitors to the White House who had been there before were immediately struck by the new atmosphere. Jack ran the Presidency; Jacqueline ran its social functions. Together they created an aura that sparkled and scintillated with intelligence and graciousness. One of those most impressed was the British Prime Minister, Harold Macmillan, who was quick to notice that something fresh and different had been added. "One of the most reassuring things about him," Mr. Macmillan said of John Kennedy, "is his capacity to change pace. He always does his homework and is always on his toes during discussions. But in the evening there will be music and fine food and good company. There is something eighteenth century about this young man. I imagine it's quite a new note in the White House."

It was indeed. The eighteenth century touch after working hours, however, was mainly Jacqueline's doing. The President left the handling of such occasions in her hands, and with sound reason. She was good at it. He also left all household decisions up to her—even when she asked for his advice. This left Jacqueline entirely on her own in such matters, as she once explained humorously to an interviewer. "When I start to ask him silly little insignificant questions," she said, ". . . about whether Caroline should appear at some reception, or whether I should wear a short or long dress, he just snaps his fingers and says, 'That's your province.' And I say, 'Yes, but you're the great decision-maker. Why should everyone but me get the benefit of your decisions?' "

There were other areas of responsibility for Jacqueline. Sometimes the President had to make official trips away from the White House. Jacqueline didn't go on too many of these with him. She thought it more important that she stay with the children. Jack agreed. A First Lady, he had once said, is a woman before she is anything else. As such she must first be a wife to her husband and a mother to her children. This was the way Jacqueline saw her role, too. The Scottish author, Thomas Carlyle, had once written that one should always do the duty that lay closest to hand. The duty that lay closest to her hand—and heart—was her duty to her children.

There was one trip though that she didn't want to miss. This was Jack's first official visit to Europe to talk politics with some of the world's leaders. France was their first major port of call, in late May, 1961. Their host was General Charles de Gaulle, President of the French Republic and one of Europe's great statesmen. An unforgettable dinner by candlelight was held in their honor in the magnificent Hall of Mirrors at the Palace of Versailles. Afterward they saw a superb ballet performance in the palace's Louis XV Theater.

Paris—wonderful Paris—always gave Jacqueline a feeling of homecoming. The Parisians, too, felt a special kinship with her. "Vive, Jacqueline!" they shouted, and the press echoed their cries. It was a unique personal triumph. Not since Napoleon had anyone made such a total conquest of this city of cities. Her gown by Givenchy and her fourteenth-century bouffant hair-do drew raves. The President and General de Gaulle did all the conferring and the speechmaking, but Jacqueline got all the headlines. The General found her charming. He usually didn't unbend to strangers and visitors. But Jacqueline completely captivated him. They spent a lot of time at receptions and dinners chatting away in French. Jack, who could barely get a word in, gracefully admitted defeat. At a press luncheon in Paris he introduced himself as "the man who accompanied Jacqueline Kennedy to Paris."

Their next big stop, in June, was Vienna. There they met Premier Nikita Khrushchev of Russia and his wife, Nina. While the two men growled at each other, the two women got along famously. They even appeared together on the balcony of the famous Schönbrun Palace and held clasped hands aloft while the friendly Viennese crowd below chanted, "Jackie! Nina!" Khrushchev was also very gallant toward Jacqueline. When a photographer at a reception asked him to shake hands with the American President, he pointed to Jacqueline and said, "I'd rather shake hands with her."

England was rather tame after all this, although the
English, who knew how to mix pomp with good manners,
put on a big show for them. Prime Minister Macmillan,
with his Colonel Blimp mustache, looked as if he'd been
born in tweeds. Queen Elizabeth and her husband Prince
Philip invited them to Buckingham Palace for dinner,
the first time its royal precincts had been invaded by an
American President since Woodrow Wilson called on
King George V in 1918. Jacqueline couldn't help thinking that the last time she had seen Queen Elizabeth was
when she had covered her coronation as a reporter for the
Washington *Times-Herald*.

Greece came next—but that was for fun and vacation.
Jack had to go back to Washington, so she and her sister
Lee, now the Princess Radziwill, toured the enchanted
isles together. It was just like old times. They went to see
the famous actors of the National Theatre of Greece in a
shattering performance of *Elektra* by Sophocles and
watched spellbound as the surging drama unfolded on
the stage. Jacqueline loved Greece—both the people and
its wonderful history. Here, in these craggy islands, democracy and western civilization had been born. Every
ancient relic they saw reminded them of the glory that
had once been Greece. The Greeks gave Jacqueline rousing welcomes wherever she went. The good townfolk of
Hydra put on a native dance—the Kalamtianos—in her

honor. The music and the rhythm were so inviting that Jacqueline joined the dancers. It was, all in all, a marvelous interlude.

On her return home she found that all the girls were now wearing their hair Paris style á la Jacqueline. The "Jackie-look" had scored again. But that was an old story. Women had started copying her clothes and coiffures as soon as she became First Lady. Her effect on the world of fashion was little short of revolutionary. The well-known Hollywood designer, Edith Head, said that she was "the greatest single influence in history." It came as no surprise to anyone when she won the title of "Best-Dressed Woman of the Year."

Best-dressed or not, she still had a family to take care of. Caroline proved her most difficult problem. There was always so much publicity surrounding her. Everything the child did seemed to wind up in the newspapers. Photographers were always lying in wait to snap pictures of her.

That first year there was a flood of Caroline pictures— on a tricycle, on a pony, on a sled, on a staircase. They were endless. It got so bad that Jacqueline cut such pictures out of magazines before she left them lying around. It was harmful, she thought, for a child to be the focus of so much attention. She would grow up thinking it was her due. And she was still too young to understand why there was all this fuss about her. Once, when a reporter asked her something about the "President," Caroline replied, "He's not the President—he's my daddy."

Jacqueline fought a running but losing battle with Pierre Salinger, the President's news secretary. Pierre didn't mind the publicity at all. Nor did he, in his man's way, think that it was too damaging to Caroline. He was for anything—well, practically anything—that gave the Kennedy administration a good "image" in the eyes of the country. Jacqueline was all for maintaining a favorable image, but not if it had to be gained at her daughter's expense. As a result, she may have gotten too protective. At the end of the year, she gave Pierre a picture of herself with a half-apologetic inscription—"From the greatest cross you have to bear."

It was hard to keep the publicity spotlight off Caroline. Anything that had to do with the First Family was news. Soon it would be baby John, Jr.'s turn. John-John, as the President called him, was a merry-eyed little fellow, bubbling over with fun and laughter. He looked like his mother, whereas Caroline was a blonde-haired, blue-eyed version of the President.

Living in the White House was a constant test of patience and endurance. But there were also some unexpectedly good things to be said about it. In the case of the Kennedys, it led, oddly enough, to a closer family life.

For the first time in their marriage, Jack was home most of the time. There had scarcely been a weekend during his last three years as Senator when he hadn't been on a trip of some sort. Now they had lunch and dinner together almost every day.

There was even talking time in the evenings—more than there had ever been—when his official day had ended. He would come upstairs to their apartment and they would have dinner together. They never—or rarely —discussed the problems of the Presidency. That was something he left downstairs, at least as far as she was concerned. Once, rather absent-mindedly, Jacqueline asked what kind of day it had been. She was startled when he started ticking off, one by one, the different "crises" that had come to his desk on that particular day. But that was a slip of the tongue on her part. Mostly they talked about other things—family, friends, books—that would help take his mind away from the enormous burdens of his job.

The President, too, liked it better this way. He had been weary to the point of exhaustion when the campaign had closed. The regular routine of the White House suited him much more. He even started to put on some weight, a sure sign of settling down. The White House, for the President of the United States, was a combination home, office and command headquarters, and it was here that he carried on the nation's business and also tried to be a husband to his wife and a father to his children.

It was always a welcome break in the day's grim doings when he got a visit from Caroline. Then there would be a chat in his office or a romp on the lawn. Sometimes her visits were right out of the blue, as when she burst in on one of the Presidential news conferences in Florida wearing a pair of her mother's high-heeled shoes. Reporters—and the President—broke into grins when they saw her. It was the high point of that particular news conference.

When John-John reached the walking stage he, too, was taken for visits to his father's office downstairs. His favorite hiding place was under the President's desk. It was sometimes quite a job getting him to come out. There was always candy waiting for the children, when they left, at the desk of Mrs. Lincoln, the President's secretary. (Mrs. Lincoln, incidentally, got tired of hearing people say that they were glad to see another Lincoln back in the White House.)

Jacqueline went out of her way to give Caroline a normal childhood. She organized a cooperative nursery school with other Washington mothers she knew. Each day the children would be taken to a different mother's house. Later the school was set up on a more formal basis at the White House. All the parents—the Kennedys included—shared expenses. When the children reached elementary school age two regular teachers were hired to teach first grade. Caroline brought her lunch to school with her, as did the other children, so she could eat with her classmates. Milk, served from a White House kitchen, was paid for by the parents.

After moving into the White House, the President and his wife rented an estate in Middleburg, Virginia. This rambling, 400-acre place, called Glen Ora, became a refuge for Jacqueline and the children. The President also spent some time there with them whenever he could. There, in a spacious, rolling setting, Jacqueline could relax and find the quiet that she wanted for herself and her children. She taught Caroline to ride, just as her mother had taught her, and took both children for rides in a pony cart through the wooded countryside.

In the winter she indulged in one of her favorite sports, riding to hounds, with some of the local, enthusiastic fox hunters. When it got out that Jacqueline liked fox hunting, the White House received some indignant letters from people who thought it a cruel sport. Jacqueline replied very politely to the letters but she didn't stop chasing "Old Horrid," as fox hunters call their sly quarry. She enjoyed it too much.

A good part of the summer was spent at Hyannis Port and Newport, and there were occasional winter visits to

Palm Beach where the Joseph P. Kennedys lived in a huge mansion. The President also liked to go off on his yacht, the *Honey Fitz,* which had been named after his maternal grandfather, John F. Fitzgerald. Nicknamed "Honey Fitz" by his cronies, his mother's father had been a colorful Boston politician who had once been mayor of that fair city. While the President sat out on deck and sunned himself, Jacqueline would go water-skiing. After John Glenn became America's first man in orbit the Kennedys invited him to Hyannis Port where he and Jacqueline put on a show of their skill and speed on water skis.

The President was also an enthusiastic sportsman. As a boy he had played football, baseball, hockey, and sailed, swam, fished and golfed. During his early days in the White House the President used to sneak off on occasion to the nearby Burning Tree Country Club for a fast round of golf. Then he hurt his back again during a tree planting ceremony in Canada and there was no more golf. He really missed it. In his beautiful small book, *That Special Grace,* about his friend John Kennedy, Benjamin Bradlee tells how the President used to stride along the fairway pretending he was Arnold Palmer or some other great golfer, depending on the shot he had to make. If it was a shot that called for delicacy or finesse, he was Julius Boros. If it required boldness or daring, he was Palmer. And when the shot came off well, he was pure John Kennedy, with a grin a mile wide that showed his complete happiness.

Jacqueline had also taken up golf, but the most outstanding thing about her game was the costumes she wore—usually capri slacks and fiery-colored shirts. It had a certain effect on the fashion industry, but it didn't do a thing for golf. She was, however, having a great effect in another, more important area—that of culture and the performing arts.

It had begun with Robert Frost reading his poem at the President's inauguration. This set the tone and style for one of the most remarkable cultural flowerings in the history of the nation's capital. Never before had the White House played host to so many great talents—writers, artists, composers, poets, actors, musicians, scientists and anyone else who did things well. In a word, the touchstone was excellence.

The White House became a place that soon, in the mind of the country and the world, stood for the very best in American life. For the first time in its history, Shakespeare was performed on its premises. A dinner was held in honor of Nobel Prize winners. Great actors gave dramatic readings, as when Fredric March read from the work of Ernest Hemingway. Great musicians gave concerts, as when the incomparable Pablo Cassals played his cello. Great dancers danced—the ballet troupe of Jerome Robbins. There were even concerts for children in the East Room, where Abigail Adams, the wife of John Adams, had once hung her laundry. For forty years, before the Kennedys moved in, there had been no Presidential box in Washington's National Theater. Now it had one.

The moving spirit behind this amazing cultural eruption was Jacqueline Kennedy. It was she who conceived of the idea, planned the programs, and then brought them into being. Why? The President explained his wife's reasons. "Her emphasis upon culture at the White House functions," he said, "is an expression of her feeling that the White House ought to be the center of excellence."

As usual, there were some critics who thought that Jacqueline was "striving" too hard to bring a sense of culture to the nation. Composer and conductor Leonard Bernstein, who knew her well, disagreed. "She does not strive," said Bernstein. "It happens automatically because that's the way she lives."

Moved to make a statement on the matter, Jacqueline said, "I don't really like to call attention to anything. I think I'm more of a private person. (But) I think everything in the White House should be the finest . . . just the best."

If this was true of the arts, and of culture generally, it should also be true of the White House itself. On her first tour of the famous residence, Jacqueline was surprised at how little it reflected the lives and times of the Presidents who had once lived there. As a result, it was empty of any feeling of history. Where was the spirit of Jefferson, Jackson, Lincoln and other great Presidents of the past? One would never know from the look of it that they and their families had ever been occupants of this great and historic house. "It looks like a house where nothing has taken place," she told her husband. "There is no trace of the past."

She was also appalled that the country's number one dwelling should be so bare of the genuine article. The house was filled with reproductions of paintings—and not good ones at that. It was also loaded with fake antiques. And there were lots of potted palms—everywhere. The whole thing offended her sense of fitness. The White House shouldn't look like a second-rate antique shop. It should have, wherever possible, the original of a painting or a piece of furniture. Its rooms should make up a panorama of Presidential history; and each room should tell a part of that story.

Jacqueline was determined to restore to the White House that sense of its great past which was now missing from it. This meant throwing out or replacing everything that was spurious and putting in their places the real thing. How would she get these genuine items? She would organize a committee of experts on such matters, get it to plan a program of restoration and then put it into effect.

This would mean, of course, an enormous effort on the part of many people. It would mean a search for objects that had vanished into the dim reaches of time and history. It would mean contacting the relatives and friends of Presidents both living and dead, and getting them to search their records, their attics and their minds for anything that might be helpful to the restoration. It would mean convincing people to give of themselves and their treasured possessions. It would also mean raising funds so that items could be purchased, when necessary, from dealers or other private persons.

The fact that Jacqueline embarked on this ambitious project was a testimony to her taste, her enthusiasm, and her willingness to work hard. Even more revealing, it showed her own deep-felt need for doing things just because they are right and should be done.

She told writer Hugh Sidey, who was doing an article on the restoration, why she was undertaking such a task. "How could I help wanting to do it?" she said. "I don't know . . . is it a reverence for beauty or for history? I guess both. I've always cared. My best friends are people

who care. I don't know . . . when you read Proust or
listen to Jack talk about history or go to Mount Vernon,
you understand. I feel strongly about the children who
come here. When I think about my own son and how to
make him turn out like his father, I think of Jack's great
sense of history."

So that was it in a nutshell—she cared. And caring, she
acted. It was as simple as that.

She took her cause and her case to the American people. The way she did it—an event in itself—was memo-
rable and dramatic. In February, 1962, Jacqueline made
a one-hour television appearance. Viewers were con-
ducted on a personal tour of the White House by the
First Lady. She also showed them what had been done so
far in the restoration and what she planned to do. At
the end of the show she appealed for public support to
the project. The response was immediate and generous.

Jacqueline had another bright thought. A lot of time
and effort had gone into restoring the White House and
she wanted the project to go on after she left. The First
Ladies who came after her might not be as interested as
she was in this kind of thing. Therefore it might be wise
to turn the job over to some official organization so that
the work could go on no matter who was in the White
House. There was no such organization, so she had one
formed—the White House Historical Association. All

future procuring of items for the refurbished mansion was now put into the hands of this newly created body. The association also published a guidebook which was sold to White House tourists. This was also Jacqueline's idea. She wanted visitors—especially the young ones—to take away with them a lasting souvenir of their tour. Few guidebooks become best-sellers. This one did. In a bare six months, 350,000 copies were sold at the price of one dollar each. Money from the sales went into the general Association fund.

The busy First Lady also did something about getting the official White House Library started up again. Once it had been a going concern but over the years it had fallen into sad neglect. A librarian, hired full time, slowly began to stock it again with valuable old books and documents. This was another part of Jacqueline's plan for making the White House an historical museum whose main theme was the Presidency. Her husband had imbued her with his own strong sense of history. She now began to bring it to life in the house that was itself the symbol and the pivot of the nation's history.

The restoration was carried out and finished—for the most part—in two years. This was a remarkable feat, considering all that had to be done. Its successful completion in so short a time was mainly due to Jacqueline's ability to take hold of the project, give it a shape and a pattern, and carry it through on all levels. It even drew praise from her normally reticent husband. "The organization of the committees," said the President, "was an impressive executive job." Then, with a touch of humor, he added, "Mrs. Kennedy displayed more executive ability than I had imagined she had."

The President had also gained personally from the venture. During her many searches through the White House for forgotten treasures, Jacqueline had found something she thought just perfect for Jack. It was a desk that had been presented to President Rutherford B. Hayes by Queen Victoria of England in 1878. The desk, a massive affair, had been made from the timbers of a British ship which had gone forth in search of Sir John Franklin's ill-fated Arctic expedition. The rescue vessel —H.M.S. *Resolute*—had itself gotten stuck in the Arctic ice in 1854. Freed by a Yankee whaling ship, it was put back in tip-top shape by the United States and given back to the British with the government's compliments. Queen Victoria had been touched by this gesture. Later, when the ship was broken up, she ordered that a desk be constructed from its timbers and sent to the President of the United States.

It was this beautiful old oaken desk that Jacqueline had found loaded down with junk. It was a little worse for wear, but she knew that Jack, an old salt who loved all things nautical, would be just mad about it. He was. It was cleaned up and moved into the President's office where it became his personal desk.

This was but one of the many precious items that Jacqueline found stored away or merely abandoned in some forgotten corner of the huge dwelling. She spent months exploring every one of its nooks and crannies and came up with some exciting and unusual finds. She was also busy tracing and tracking down pieces that had once been in the White House and then had disappeared. Her bird-dogging tactics sometimes led her far afield, sometimes just around the corner. One time it led right into the Senate office of Vice-President Lyndon Johnson.

Hanging in the Vice-President's office, Jacqueline learned, was a beautiful chandelier that years ago had been a White House showpiece. There was an amusing story about why it had been removed. Its constant tinkling, so it was said, had gotten on President Theodore Roosevelt's nerves. Always a man to enjoy a little joke, the ex-Rough Rider had the offending fixture taken out and sent over to the Vice-President so that it would annoy him instead and also keep him from falling asleep on the job. True or not, after Jacqueline found out what had happened to it, she had it moved right back. Of course she first had to get the permission of the Vice-President and also the majority and minority leaders of the

Senate. All three of these gentlemen graciously gave their consent and the tinkling chandelier was returned to its rightful home.

Similar stories about Jacqueline's relentless pursuit of bygone treasures became legion. If they proved one thing, it was that there were two strong wills at work in the White House. One of her friends, marveling at her ability to keep track of all the details, said that she had "the same kind of mind the President has, in a female way." Anyone who knew the President knew that this was a compliment of the highest order.

Something else was emerging from all this. If Jacqueline disliked fakes and reproductions, so too did the American people. It was by now quite clear that in the person of their new First Lady they had a striking original. Some even rated her as one of the greatest in American history. This judgment of her role came from many distinguished quarters. Robert Frost spoke for all of them when he said about Jacqueline, "There have been some great wives in the White House—like Abigail Adams and Dolley Madison—so great that you can't think of their husbands, Presidents, without thinking of *them*. It looks as though we're having another one now." This was pretty select company and poet Frost was not in the habit of making such statements lightly.

Jacqueline was naturally pleased to have such nice

things said about her. It was also very flattering to be classed with the two illustrious ladies to whom she had been likened by the craggy old New England poet. She hadn't expected such praise, nor had she sought it. What she had done she had done simply and naturally because it was in her nature to do these things. The best and greatest of First Ladies had always been themselves, but what they had brought to their roles was the best *of* themselves. Jacqueline had therefore decided right from the start to trust herself and her own instincts. It had paid off handsomely.

Her success as First Lady was way beyond her, or anyone else's, expectations. Her trips abroad had been spectacular triumphs. At home her efforts had met with equal favor. The size of her personal mail—from all over the world—was enormous. It poured into Washington like an avalanche, averaging between six thousand and nine thousand letters a week. She even got approving and admiring correspondence from behind the Iron Curtain. No wonder members of the diplomatic corps called her "the Number One Lady Good Will Ambassador."

The President was of course delighted that his wife was held in such high esteem. Being President was a hard enough job without having to worry about whether or not people liked the First Lady. During his first two years in office Jack Kennedy had had his own ups and downs like any other President. Through it all—the good and the bad—he had kept his head and his humor. It hadn't hurt a bit either having a wife by his side who did him proud in public and also lent him moral support when he needed it. They balanced each other out perfectly in a partnership that was notable for its style and grace. Rarely in American history had there been a couple in the White House so young, so attractive, so popular, and so in tune with their times. The youth of the Kennedys was accented again in April, 1963, when the announcement came from the White House that Jacqueline was pregnant again.

In this third year of his Presidency, John F. Kennedy faced the future with hope and firm resolve. There was still much for him to do. The peace of the world was still a fragile thing that could be shattered by the press of a button. Above all other things he had set himself the goal of keeping and preserving the peace, somehow to find a way out of the blind alley of an atomic war that threatened the whole human race. On August 5, he took a giant step in the direction of this dream when a nuclear test ban treaty was signed by the United States and Russia.

Good news was followed swiftly by bad, this time of a personal nature. On August 7, Jacqueline, summering at Hyannis Port, was rushed to the nearby Otis Air Force Base Hosital. Informed in Washington, the President flew there at once. The baby, born prematurely, lived for only two days. Doctors tried all they knew how to save his life. When tiny Patrick Bouvier Kennedy was buried at the Brookline Cemetery in Boston, the President wept for his dead son.

Worn out from her ordeal, Jacqueline needed a change of scene and mood. The doctors had ordered her to take a rest but she did not rush into it. She wanted to spend some time first with her husband and her children. Physically, she recovered quickly, but sorrow takes longer to heal. At Glen Ora she watched the leaves take on their autumn colors. Then, as the hunters' horns called the hounds to the chase again, she was off on a two-week jaunt, again with sister Lee, to Greece and the fabled lands of the Mediterranean. It was an idyll without time against the measureless spaces of sun and sea in countries as old as antiquity. When she returned to the White House to resume her duties as First Lady, she found that politics had again become the order of the day.

Somewhere around the end of the third year of his first term a President becomes aware that soon he will be running for reelection if nominated again by his party. There was no question that John F. Kennedy would be his party's standard bearer again in 1964. The only thing in doubt was who the Republicans would put up to run against him. Not that anyone was really too keen to get

that assignment. The President, in spite of certain diffi-
culties, was considered unbeatable. Even so, John F.
Kennedy, a political pro to the core, was taking no
chances.

Like a skillful fencer who likes to warm up with a few
practice thrusts, he began to make some swift political
sorties. The object of these journeys was to get a firsthand
feel of the temper of the people. The South was his
greatest problem. Emotions were running high there
against his civil rights program. After a hundred years of
legal freedom the Negro was still trying to become a full
man. The President did not expect to carry the South in
the next election. But he thought that some southern
states, like Florida and Texas, might fall into his lap if he
played his cards right. On November 18, he made
speeches in two Florida cities, Tampa and Miami Beach.
Later that same week he planned a full-scale assault on
the state of Texas. He had another good reason for going
to Texas. There was a serious political split in the state's
Democratic party and the President wanted to help patch
up the rift.

Jacqueline usually didn't accompany the President on
such trips. But she had once promised Vice-President
Lyndon Johnson, a native Texan, that she would visit his
home state some day. The Vice-President reminded her
of this promise and Jacqueline agreed to go. Lyndon

Johnson and his wife, Lady Bird, would also be making the journey with them. On November 21, the invasion of Texas began. It was a smashing success. The President and his wife were greeted by cheering crowds in San Antonio, Houston and Fort Worth. Again Jacqueline—just as she had been in Paris and other places—was the hit of the show. The President was exhilarated by the wonderful receptions. He hadn't expected such demonstrations of warmth and friendship. Texas was supposed to be angry about the civil rights issue. There were also lots of right-wing groups in Texas which disliked the President and his administration. But if all of Texas was going to be like this he couldn't wait to see more.

They spent the night in a Fort Worth hotel. The next day, Friday, November 22, they were scheduled to fly to another Texas city on their itinerary—Dallas.

Dallas
CHAPTER EIGHT

John F. Kennedy went to bed that night looking forward to another day of triumph. Some of his advisers, though, were a little worried about Dallas. It might be the toughest nut of all to crack. This hotbed of right-wing extremism had already boiled over twice before in bad temper and violence. During the 1960 campaign Vice-President Johnson and his wife had been roughed up by an unruly mob in the lobby of a Dallas hotel. Then, only last month, the Ambassador to the United Nations, Adlai Stevenson, had been insulted and spat upon by a gang of Dallas demonstrators. Both these incidents were worrisome signs, but the President was by nature an optimistic man. And a brave one. He himself had made the decision not to avoid the city. He would go to Dallas.

The next morning he was the first one up and the first one out. He was eager to get the day going. It didn't look too promising. The skies over Fort Worth were clouded over and a light drizzle was falling, not the best kind of weather for a politician going out to meet the people.

Jacqueline was getting herself ready for the day at a more leisurely pace. When the President left their suite they agreed to rendezvous at a breakfast being tendered for them by the Fort Worth Chamber of Commerce in this very hotel. Flanked by Secret Service men, John Kennedy rode down the elevator and then walked through the lobby out into the street. Through a fine mist of rain he strode across the street to a parking lot jam-packed with Texans who were waiting to see him. Smiling and shaking hands, he made his way slowly along the edge of the crowd.

Someone cried, "Where's Jackie?" and others took up the refrain. The President's face broke into a grin. "Mrs. Kennedy," he told them, "is busy organizing herself. It takes a little longer, but then she looks so much better than we do."

The people were so friendly that he had a hard time tearing himself away. A politician always hates to leave when he's got an audience in the palm of his hand. But it was time to go. He was already late for the Chamber of Commerce breakfast. He waved his good-byes and crossed the street back into the hotel.

The President was chatting amiably with some local Fort Worth citizens around the breakfast table when Jacqueline walked in. The First Lady was a positive vision in a suit of shocking pink and the pertest of hats to match. Fort Worth hadn't seen anything so fresh and lovely out of Washington since as far back as it could remember. The buzz of talk at the tables stopped as if someone had thrown a switch. There was a burst of spontaneous applause. When the President got to his feet to make a short speech he was in a light, bantering mood. "Two years ago," he began, "I introduced myself in Paris by saying that I was the man who had accompanied Mrs. Kennedy to Paris. I am getting somewhat the same sensation as I travel around Texas. Nobody wonders what Lyndon and I wear."

It was true. All the crowds so far had reserved their loudest Texas yells for Jacqueline. The President was delighted for personal *and* political reasons. In their suite the night before he had told his wife that her presence in Texas would mean thousands of votes for him in next year's election. That meant he was extra glad she had come along.

Now, as he finished his remarks and walked out, arm in arm with Jacqueline, the Chamber gave them a rousing send-off. The charm of the Kennedys had captured another stronghold. Before leaving for the airport, the President conferred briefly with Vice-President Johnson. He wanted the Vice-President to know how pleased he was with the way things were working out. "Well, Lyndon," he said jovially, "we'll carry two states anyway— Texas and Massachusetts." The Vice-President was heartened, too. He'd been a little worried about how his native state would receive the President. But after all this his worries were down to practically zero.

They drove out to the airport in brilliant sunshine. The weather had cleared and the day had turned sunny and warm. There were the usual good-byes, mostly official. Then the Kennedys and their entourage and the Johnsons and theirs took to the air in separate planes. The flight to Dallas didn't take long. The Vice-President and Lady Bird left first aboard the *Air Force Two*. The President and Jacqueline followed five minutes later in the Presidential plane, *Air Force One*. They touched down at Love Field, in Dallas, at 11:40 A.M. As the Presi-

dent and his wife stepped to the ground someone handed
the First Lady a large bouquet of red roses. For a moment Jacqueline thought this odd. These were the first
red roses she had seen in Texas. All the other welcoming
groups had presented her with yellow roses. For some
strange reason the change bothered her. She kept thinking about it as they greeted the crowd behind the airport
fence and then got into the limousine that was to take
them into the city of Dallas. As she and Jack sat down in
the rear of the car she placed the bouquet down beside
her so that it lay between them on the seat.

The Presidential limousine usually came equipped
with a clear plastic bubbletop. But today, because of the
beautiful weather, the bubbletop had been removed.
The President's party also included Governor John Connally of Texas and his wife Nellie. The Governor and
Mrs. Connally sat on jump seats directly in front of the
President and Jacqueline. It was 11:50 A.M. when the
motorcade left the airport for Dallas. A winding eleven-
mile route lay ahead of it before it would reach the city's
Trade Mart where the President was scheduled to deliver
a speech against "voices preaching . . . that vitupera-
tion is as good as victory and that peace is a sign of weak-
ness."

Much precaution is taken by the Secret Service and the
local police when the President of the United States

drives through the crowded streets of a city. This motorcade, like all others, was organized in precise fashion to
insure maximum protection for the Chief Executive. A
squad of Dallas motorcycle police headed the motorcade.
Then came a car filled with members of the Dallas police
force, followed by more police on motorcycles. Next in
line, four or five car lengths in front of the Presidential
limousine, rode the "rolling command car," so called
because its passengers were made up of the Dallas chief of
police, two Secret Service agents, and the sheriff of Dallas
county. Any suspicious movement or action noted by
these forward units would bring instant response by
armed police and Secret Service men. Normally, there
would also be Secret Service agents running alongside, or
riding on the running boards of the President's car, but
the President had requested that they not be used this
time. His wishes were obeyed. To the rear of the limousine, however, flanking it on either side, were four more
motorcycles. Another car, filled with armed Secret Service agents and two of the President's personal assistants,
followed directly behind it. The Vice-President's car,
trailed by more motorcycles and official vehicles, completed the motorcade.

This security arrangement had been worked out by the
Secret Service during its many years of protecting Presidents. But as the President himself had said only that

same morning to his aide Kenneth O'Donnell, ". . . if anybody really wanted to shoot the President of the United States, it was not a very difficult job—all one had to do was get a high building some day with a telescopic rifle, and there was nothing anybody could do to defend against such an attempt."

As the motorcade moved through the outskirts of Dallas, the crowds lining the streets were sparse. Twice the President brought the procession to a halt to chat with some of the people along the way. Once it was to shake hands with someone who held a sign asking him to stop and shake hands. The sign-holder was overwhelmed when the President did just that. Another time he paused to speak briefly with a nun and a group of small children in her charge. There were no more unscheduled stops. When the downtown section of the city hove into view the streets were suddenly packed so solid and tight it was hard to pick out a single face.

Now the police had their work cut out for them. Trying to keep the crowds back was like trying to plug up a leaky dam. People kept surging out into the street and had to be pushed back constantly. No sooner was one human wave turned aside than there was another one to deal with. Secret Service agents jumped out of the car behind the President's and ran forward to take up protective positions on both sides of the limousine. Every

time someone moved toward the President he was un-
ceremoniously shoved away. Once a teenage boy dashed
toward the rear of the car. Only the quick action of an
agent prevented him from climbing aboard.

The police and the Secret Service were having their
hands full, but the President was enjoying himself. The
roar of the crowd was music to his ears. This was by far
the biggest turnout they'd had so far. And to think it
should be Dallas! John Kennedy kept smiling and waving. To his left, Jacqueline too was acknowledging the
loud acclaim with smiles and waves. She tried to keep her
mind off the heat and the sun. It was furnace-hot inside
their open car. The sun had been beating squarely down
on them ever since they had left the airport. She couldn't
wait to get out of it, to some place that was cool.

As they left Main Street and then turned another
corner she saw that the crowd was thinning out. They
passed a huge square building—the Texas School Book
Depository—and bore left in a sweeping turn. Then,
straight ahead, glory be, she spied an underpass. It would
be cool under there!

She heard Nellie Connally, the Governor's wife, say to
Jack, "Mr. President, you can't say that Dallas doesn't
love you." Jack's reply, "No, you can't. . . ."—or—
"That is very obvious. . . ." was lost in all the clapping
and cheering.

Jacqueline kept facing to the left, still smiling, still waving, still hot. Then there was a sound like a car or a motorcycle backfiring, no different it seemed from the other noises in a motorcade. A shout of "Oh, no, no, no." from Governor Connally made her whirl sharply to the right. There sat Jack, slightly slumped over, with an odd, puzzled look on his face. His left hand appeared to be holding his throat. Then there was another barking sound, this time flat and ugly. Without a word, Jack brushed a hand to his forehead and fell over into her lap.

The cry that came from Jacqueline was like something torn out of her flesh. "Oh, no, no!" she screamed. "Oh, my God, they have killed my husband. Jack, Jack! I love you, Jack!"

She turned, in her grief and terror, to seek help—something. There, behind her, she saw a figure starting to climb up the back of the car. Dazed and unseeing, she clambered toward him, up over the seat onto the rear deck, reaching with her hand. The man—Special Agent Clint Hill—pushed her back into the car. When he finally got in himself she was sitting there with the President in her lap, face up, sobbing, "Jack, Jack, what have they done to you?"

Hill could also hear the radio in the car crackling, "To the nearest hospital, quick. We have been hit."

Like a wounded whippet the limousine sped off. Motorcycle sirens wailed ahead of it, leading the way to the hospital. Jacqueline sat silently now, bent over her stricken husband, cradling him in her arms. From up front she heard Nellie Connally crying. Then she knew —or suspected—that the Governor too had been shot. How seriously she didn't know. As for Jack, there was little hope in her heart. She was sure he was dead.

The limousine got to Parkland General Hospital— four miles away—in about nothing flat. The shooting had occurred at 12:30 P.M. It was 12.35 P.M. when the sleek Lincoln pulled up at the hospital's Emergency entrance. Men in white, already alerted, raced out with stretchers, one for the President, another for the Governor. As they carried Jack's body inside, Jacqueline followed. Her pink suit, no longer immaculate, was stained with blood. So were her stockings, her shoes, her hands. In the emergency room she stood by watching as the doctors began working feverishly on Jack. There was still the barest flicker of life in that valiant body but it was going out fast. Knowing it was all hopeless, like someone awake inside a nightmare, Jacqueline went outside to wait and to pray.

Shortly before one o'clock, last rites were administered to the President by Father Huber, a Catholic priest. At one o'clock the President of the United States was pronounced dead. He had been shot twice. The first bullet had struck him in the neck, the second in the back of the head. Doctors said he could have recovered from the first wound; the second, however, had proved fatal. Governor Connally had been luckier. His wound, though serious, had not struck any vital organs. He would recover.

News had already come in over the radio that the shots had been fired from the Texas School Book Depository, the building they had passed just before driving toward the underpass. As the afternoon progressed there were further reports. An alarm had been broadcast with a description of the suspected assassin. Just before two o'clock the suspect was seized and arrested in a movie theater. His name was Lee Harvey Oswald. He was also thought to have shot and killed a Dallas patrolman, J. D. Tippit, shortly before his arrest.

Through all this, Jacqueline sat and waited with the body of her slain husband. They tried to get her to leave the room for a while, to go somewhere to rest or lie down. She would not go. Doctors offered her medical sedation to help quiet her nerves. She would not take any. She wanted nothing but to be with her husband, to stay with him until the casket came. When it came and the body was placed inside she took his limp hand in hers and slipped her wedding ring on his finger. She wanted to give him something that she loved. It was the only thing she could think of.

She went along, too, when the casket was put into an

ambulance and driven out to the airport. Agent Clint Hill and Admiral Burkley, the White House physician, accompanied her on this short trip. As they sat quietly inside the ambulance, Dr. Burkley handed Jacqueline two red roses. He had found them inside the President's shirt. Then Jacqueline remembered the bouquet in the car, the one she had been given that morning at the airport, the red roses that had then seemed so strange to her because they were not yellow like the ones she had received in all the other Texas cities they had visited. And here now were two of them come back to her with redder leaves than ever roses had before.

Air Force One was ready for takeoff when they got to Love Field. Already aboard was the new President of the United States, Lyndon Johnson. He had been waiting for Jacqueline to arrive before starting the flight back to Washington. The bronze casket was placed in the rear of the plane. At 2:38 the new President was sworn in by an old friend, Judge Sarah T. Hughes, who had been whisked out to the airport to administer the oath of office. Standing by, among others, were Jacqueline and the President's wife, Lady Bird. When he had finished the oath with the words, ". . . so help me God," Lyndon Johnson kissed his wife. Then he turned to Jacqueline, put his arm around her, and kissed her gently on the cheek. Ten minutes later the huge jet was airborne.

Cruising at an altitude of 41,000 feet, it gunned its way northward at a speed of 625 miles an hour.

The flight to Washington took a little over two hours. All that time Jacqueline sat next to the casket in the plane's rear lounge. Occasionally she was joined by one of the late President's assistants, men like Kenneth O'Donnell, David Powers, and Lawrence O'Brien, who had known John Kennedy as boss and friend and had loved him dearly. They came to sit and share her vigil, sometimes to speak brief words of comfort or simply to sit in silence and give her the strength and warmth of another human presence.

Evening had fallen softly over the nation's capital when *Air Force One* landed at Andrews Air Force Base. A change in time zone clocked the landing in at 5:59 P.M., eastern standard time. Waiting for Jacqueline and John F. Kennedy was the dead President's brother, Attorney General Robert F. Kennedy. Now, as always, when she needed him most, Bobby was there, just as he would be in the days to come and afterward. They stood together, hand in hand, watching the casket come out of the plane and then move, on a yellow truck, toward a waiting Navy ambulance. Then they both got into the ambulance and drove to the Bethesda Naval Hospital where an official examination would be made of the body before it was made ready for burial.

It was not quite dawn when the same ambulance drove up the White House driveway. An honor guard of Marines lifted out a flag-draped coffin and bore it solemnly toward the silent mansion. Walking behind it came Jacqueline, Bobby, and other members of the Kennedy family. They followed it to the East Room of the White House where it would lie in repose throughout the following day.

Jacqueline Kennedy had brought her husband home.

Portrait in Courage
CHAPTER NINE

The death of a President is always a shock. It is doubly so when the President is struck down suddenly and savagely by a cowardly, unseen assassin. The death of John F. Kennedy had the impact of a giant earthquake tremor. In an instant—the single flicker of an eyelash— everything had been turned upside down. The nation and the world went numb with horror, dumb with dis-

belief. More than a President had died with John F.
Kennedy. Youth had died—faith—hope—belief—the future. It is a sad thing when an old President dies. But the
death of a young President at the peak of his gifts and
powers is sadder by far. Never before in history had the
whole world, friend and foe alike, stopped what it was
doing to weep and grieve for a single man.

In London they stood in the rain outside the American
Embassy and cried. In Berlin they walked by torchlight
in the predawn dark. In Ireland they cried the night
away, and then the day. In Dallas they placed wreaths on
the spot where John F. Kennedy had died. Everywhere—
behind the Iron Curtain too—they mourned the death of
the young President.

Their thoughts turned, too, to the woman who had sat
beside him when the assassin's bullets struck. What of
her, his widowed wife, the mother of his two small children, this lovely, gay, shy, exquisite girl who must now
take up all the burdens of all the days ahead alone? They
could not forget her cries of anguish, the sight of her with
a dying President in her arms, her blood-spattered clothes
and her eyes already haunted with the look of a wound
too deep to ever heal. How would she—how could she—
pass through this ordeal that was beyond flesh and spirit
to endure?

Society reporter Cholly Knickerbocker had once written of Jacqueline that she had the "daintiness of porcelain." Her friend William Walton knew better. She might look dainty and fragile but there was a vein of iron at the core of her. A "strong dame" he had called her—and meant it. That strength was now to show itself in a performance so remarkable that it touched the heart and the pride of all who witnessed it. Even the bizarre sequel to the tragedy that was to occur in Dallas on Sunday, November 24—the assassination of the suspected assassin by a man named Jack Ruby—could not take away from the aura of majesty and dignity which Jacqueline brought to the final act of this terrible drama.

She had started making her plans for the funeral on the plane trip back to Washington. It was then, while sitting quietly beside her husband's casket, that she had had her first real chance to think in a clear-headed way. Jack was not here now to guide her with his cool, logical mind. Yet it was he who had helped her find the answer in a sense of duty so strong that it overshadowed all other things, even her sorrow. Still in shock, still groping to find her way back to reason and meaning, she had simply thought of what he would do in her place—what he would want her to do for him and for the country. He was dead, but she still lived. He must live now through her and she through him.

Her mind turned to Abraham Lincoln, another martyred President who had met death at the hands of an assassin. His funeral had been an event that had gone down in history. This was what Jack's must be, too. The Presidency had to be restored to its full sense of power and greatness. It could not be allowed to lie soiled in the dust where it had fallen. The shame of Dallas had to be wiped out. An American President had died by violence. Now he must be buried with the honor, the dignity, the respect befitting that office. This was the task that lay before her now. This was the deed she owed her husband, the duty she owed her country.

The first message she sent from *Air Force One* went to the Bethesda Naval Hospital in Maryland. She was bringing the body of the ex-PT boat skipper there to be prepared for burial. After she brought it to Bethesda she waited through the long night and morning until it was ready for its journey to the White House. She did not waste her time at Bethesda. Already the wheels of ceremony and ritual were being set in motion by this indomitable woman of pride and purpose.

She had learned a lot about the Presidency and its history while restoring the White House. That knowledge was now put to good use as she began to plan the events of the next three days. Jack was to lie in state first at the White House on Saturday. Then, on Sunday, his body would be taken to the rotunda of the Capitol for public viewing. The funeral would take place on Monday. She wanted every detail of the ceremonies to match those of Lincoln's as closely as possible. A friend was sent to get a book about Lincoln from one of the White House libraries. She had remembered that there were drawings and photographs in this particular volume which showed the different aspects of Lincoln's lying-in-state and funeral.

There was no rest for her that night. On Saturday morning, back at the White House, she was still hard at work in the East Room, seeing to it that her instructions and wishes were carried out. After that was done, there remained the hardest task of all—to tell the children. It was getting close to noon when Jacqueline Kennedy finally allowed herself the luxury of some sleep.

But there is never any real rest for the weary. Sunday afternoon it began again. The day was bright with sun but cold. A caisson drawn by six white horses came to the White House for the President's coffin. Jacqueline and her two children, Caroline and John-John, stood at the North Portico watching the honor guard carry it out. Then the cortege began its slow procession, out the White House grounds, and through the streets of Washington to the Capitol. Hundreds of thousands had come out to watch it pass and pay it silent homage. Three Presidents had come this way before on the same caisson—Abraham Lincoln in 1865, James Garfield in 1881, and Franklin D. Roosevelt in 1945. John F. Kennedy was the fourth.

When Lincoln's body had traveled this route in April, 1865, a newspaper had written: "The procession which escorted the body from the White House to the Capitol was one of the most imposing ever seen in Washington . . . The avenue was cleared the whole length. . . . The sound of muffled drums was heard, and the procession, with slow and measured tread, moved from the home of mourning on its mission with the remains of the illustrious dead. Despite the enormous crowd the silence was profound." A modern reporter might easily have written the same description, word for word, about the Kennedy cortege almost a hundred years later.

At the Capitol the pallbearers carried the coffin up the marble steps—thirty-six in all. Here Jacqueline had added a personal touch. The Navy had meant a lot to Jack. So now, for the young naval lieutenant who had fought for his country in the Pacific, she had the Navy hymn sung while his coffin was borne into the rotunda. There it was placed on the same catafalque that had held the body of Lincoln. Family, guests and dignitaries stood in a circle inside the huge circular chamber. Two Presidents were there, standing near Jacqueline. One was the new President, Lyndon Johnson. The other was an old

President, Harry Truman. Above them all, Presidents and plain people, there loomed the soaring Capitol dome, shooting shafts of dust-streaked sunlight down into the cavernous room. Everywhere they looked they could see the mighty American past staring back at them from paintings and sculpture. It was a room filled with history. More was being made now.

First to speak was Senator Mike Mansfield of Montana, the Majority Leader of the Senate. His tribute to the fallen President, and to Jacqueline, was touching and eloquent. For a moment, under the impact of his words, Jacqueline swayed. Then she righted herself and stood quietly again. Behind her veil there was a glint of tears but never more than a glint. When the Senator had finished she gave him the flicker of a smile in thanks.

There were more speeches, more words, solemn with the weight of the occasion. Their echoes rang hollowly against the arching, vaulting walls, hung ghostlike in the air, then fell apart and drifted away. When the last word was said there was a silence louder than sound. A wreath from President Johnson was placed at the foot of the bier. Jacqueline and six-year-old Caroline knelt briefly before the casket and said a prayer. When they got up to leave, the formal ceremony was over. The curious, roving eyes of the television cameras had watched it all. Now the people would be let in to pay their respects. Some

250,000 of them came all day and night and far into the morning.

Around nine in the evening Jacqueline and Bob Kennedy returned to the rotunda. Jacqueline had wanted to come again, so Bobby took her. He stood aside while she walked over to the casket, knelt, and placed her lips to the flag. Then she and Bobby walked out together into the cold night air, past the shuffling line of people who were filing in. A car was waiting for them, but Jacqueline spurned it. "Let me walk, let me walk," she said to Bobby. He let her go, following slowly behind. A woman waiting in line recognized her. She left her place impulsively, went over to Jacqueline and put her arms around her. Jacqueline returned the embrace and the two women stood there silently, needing no words to tell each other what they felt. Then the woman, just as quietly, went back to her place and Jacqueline walked on. More people spoke words of sympathy as she passed by. Word spread that it was Jacqueline and a crowd started to gather. Secret Service agents went quickly to get her. They brought her back to the car. As soon as she got in, it drove off to the White House.

One more day remained of her official ordeal. Then the curtain would be rung down and it would be over, at least this public part of it. Then she could go back to the nighttime quiet of her private grief.

The sniper in Dallas had done more than kill a President. He had left a living wound in the heart of the country. Monday had been declared a day of national mourning by President Johnson. Americans everywhere stayed home to watch a President go to his final resting place. John F. Kennedy was to be buried at Arlington, the national cemetery of heroes.

Jacqueline had chosen Arlington over the Kennedy family plot in Massachusetts because, as she said, "He belongs to the country." She may also have recalled what Jack had said one day last spring on a visit to Arlington. He had gone there with a friend to get away for a while from the cares of his office. From the rolling green slopes he had looked out across the Potomac toward the sweeping vista of Washington beyond it and said, almost wistfully, "I could stay here forever." He would now have his wish.

The great of the earth had come to Washington to see him off on his last journey. Kings and queens, presidents and prime ministers, princes and potentates—they were all there from every country in the world. Now, as the morning moved toward noon, they waited at the White House for the funeral cortege to arrive from the Capitol. When it did, they went to join it. Its first stop, before going on to Arlington, would be St. Matthew's Cathedral.

Shortly before the procession began again there was

another scare. The Central Intelligence Agency had good reason to believe that an attempt might be made on the life of General de Gaulle of France. Learning of the threat, Jacqueline sent word to the General asking that he ride instead of walk to the Cathedral. General de Gaulle's reply was typical of this great soldier and statesman. He thanked Jacqueline for being so considerate. Nevertheless, he would walk with the others. He had come to the United States to honor President Kennedy whom he had likened to a "soldier fallen in battle." He would see this duty through, threat or no threat.

When the procession left the White House grounds the tall figure of de Gaulle, attired in a simple undecorated uniform, was plainly visible, towering above the marchers. In front of the foreign contingent, a few yards to the rear of Jacqueline and the Kennedy family, marched President Lyndon Johnson and his wife, Lady Bird. The march to the Cathedral had been Jacqueline's idea. "What if it rains?" someone had asked. "Then we'll march under umbrellas," had been her reply.

Behind the caisson there pranced a riderless horse led by an army enlisted man. The name of this beautiful, spirited animal, fittingly enough, was Black Jack. As he trotted along, pawing and pulling, and occasionally rearing, the crowd along the way could see that the boots in his gleaming silver stirrups were reversed, a sign that his rider was dead.

At St. Matthew's the procession came to a halt. Caroline and John-John, who had been driven there, got out to join their mother. When John-John saw the church he began to cry. His mother shushed him and he soon grew quiet. When they went inside a friend stayed with him in the rear, amusing the child by showing him pictures in religious booklets.

The flag-draped coffin had been carried inside and set down before the altar. The mourners listened in hushed silence as Richard Cardinal Cushing of Boston said low funeral mass for his dead President and friend. Ten years ago it had been this same raspy-voiced, warm-hearted prelate who had married Jack Kennedy and Jacqueline Bouvier. Now he had come to utter words of another kind. In the midst of the solemn service he was suddenly moved to refer to the President in personal terms as "dear Jack." Here Jacqueline could hold her tears back no longer.

Afterward, as she stood on the steps of the Cathedral watching the coffin go back on the caisson, she was dry-eyed again and composed. Her children stood beside her. It was, sad to say, John-John's third birthday. As John F. Kennedy's casket went by him, the little boy raised his hand to his forehead in a last salute to his father.

Now it was time to go to Arlington. The children were sent home. Jacqueline wanted to spare them at least this. The walkers now took to cars, driving slowly behind the caisson and its six horses. It took an hour for the short journey to be completed. At Arlington fifty jets roared overhead in thundering homage. Then came *Air Force One,* the Presidential plane, dipping its wings as it went by. Cardinal Cushing said a last prayer. Cannons boomed from the hills twenty-one times. There was the sharp crackle of a rifle volley, then the mournful notes of taps. The flag covering the coffin was lifted off and folded by the honor guard. It was given to Jacqueline. Her eyes brimmed over as she took it. Bobby Kennedy, who had stood at her side through all this, was there again to lead her away. They drove back to the White House together.

There was still one last formal rite to be gone through. It showed Jacqueline at her gracious best. Many dignitaries had come from far-off lands to honor her husband. Now she would receive them at her apartment in the White House and thank each one of them personally. By five o'clock it was finished. John F. Kennedy's First Lady had performed her last official act.

This was not a day to celebrate John-John's birthday, but she had not forgotten that her son had just turned three. A little after six o'clock she called Dave Powers, Jack's loyal assistant, and asked him to come up to the Presidential apartment. Powers, normally a merry, lively Irishman, was still bowed down with grief. It had been he who had entertained the President with his humor and his wonderful storytelling ability. Jack had liked him so much that he had even invited him along on his nightly swims in the White House pool. Now Jacqueline asked him to do something for Jack's son, to play with him so that he would have some fun on his birthday. Powers understood. Soon the two—the big Irishman and the little Kennedy boy—were marching up and down in a noisy game of soldiers.

Jacqueline could not sleep that night without saying good-bye again to Jack. At midnight she returned to Arlington with Bobby. She had brought a sprig of fresh flowers to leave behind. Next day she took Caroline to visit her father's grave.

All over the country and the world people marveled at this woman who had carried her burden with so much grace and dignity. Those who had scoffed before now rose to cheer. One lady reporter who had been among the doubters now wrote: "I always thought that there was nothing Mrs. Kennedy did that I couldn't have done better. I was wrong. I couldn't have gone through that funeral. For the first time I find myself using words like 'heroine' with a straight face."

Those on the inside were just as admiring. Members of the late President's staff had shared these tragic days with her and knew better than anyone else the full measure of her valor. "Mrs. Kennedy carried us through," said one of them. ". . . She kept so many of us from falling apart."

They had caught their first glimpse of this spirit at Dallas. After the first shock had worn off, Jacqueline had become bitter with anger at the brutal, senseless act that had robbed her of a husband and the country of a President. Then, on the flight back to Washington, still groggy and dazed, she had begun to fight her way back. She had also found time to worry about others, about all those, for instance, who had worked for Jack so long and so well and were now faced with uncertain futures. To Dave Powers, Ken O'Donnell and Larry O'Brien, who had made the flight back with her, she had said, "What's to become of all of you? What are you going to do?"

At Bethesda, where she had sat and waited through the grim hours for her husband's body, both this fierceness and gentle concern about others was also visible. When someone suggested that she remove the blood-stained suit which she was still wearing, she refused. "It's his blood . . ." she had said firmly, as if this was explanation enough. Then she had turned to Mrs. Evelyn Lincoln, Jack's grief-stricken secretary, and said solicitously and even with a touch of humor, "It's getting late and I'm going to be here for a while, so why don't you go home and try to get some rest? You hold up for the next few days, and then we'll all collapse."

She had also not forgotten another widow thousands of miles away. On Saturday, the day after the assassination, she had asked Bobby to call the wife of J. D. Tippit, the murdered Dallas police officer, and express their sympathies. "What that poor woman must be going through," she had said.

Professional politicians refer to themselves as *pols,* which is short for politicians. They are a hard breed, geared to trouble and disaster, and they don't panic easily. One of them, Larry O'Brien, put it this way about Jacqueline: "We were supposed to be the tough pols, but this frail girl turned out to have more strength than any of us."

Jack Kennedy had known this all along about his wife. "My wife," he had once said, "is a very strong woman . . . romantic by temperament, sensitive, intuitive."

Her mother, Mrs. Hugh Auchincloss, rounded out the portrait. Jacqueline, she said, "has a marvelous self-control and discipline, which conceals a certain inner tension. She feels very strongly, very intensely about things."

All these qualities had now been put on full display under circumstances without equal in history. Jacqueline had done what she had set out to do, for as columnist Mary McGrory wrote in the Washington *Evening Star,* "It has been as though she were trying to show the world that courtesy and courage did not die at Dallas."

More than that, she had shown it that the human spirit when sorely tried can not only survive but rise to heights of greatness. In a letter to Jacqueline—one of 800,000 she got in the weeks after Dallas—a woman, newly widowed herself, spoke for everyone with these words: "Your self-possession and dignity in the last few days have strengthened us, for you have told us eloquently that we can prevail in the face of the greatest disaster."

Those days, like the trials of Job, had now come to an end, leaving a legend in their wake. In this longest weekend of her life, Jacqueline had held the center of the world stage. Now she had left it to go back to—what? What would the days ahead bring for this woman still in the full bloom of her beauty and youth? Dallas had been a watershed in her life. Was it just an end to something or also a new beginning? These were questions that only time would answer. One thing was certain—she would not sit around feeling sorry for herself or wait for the future to come to her. Already she was busy gathering up the threads of existence again.

There were her children to raise, and they had always been more important to her than anything else. There was also her husband's memory and her dedication to keeping it alive. Honor would come to John F. Kennedy in every way and everywhere after his death. Schools, towns, streets, bridges, plazas were named after him. Idle-

wild Airport in New York became Kennedy Airport.
Cape Canaveral in Florida was renamed Cape Kennedy.
Monuments were erected, memorials inscribed. An un-
climbed peak in Canada (which brother Bobby later
scaled) was named Mount Kennedy. And what the Kennedy family—and Jacqueline—hoped would be his
greatest monument was taking shape on the planning
boards: the John F. Kennedy Memorial Library which
would rise in the very shadow of Harvard University
along Boston's Charles River.

There would be many such honors, many monuments,
in Paris, London, Rome, Berlin and other capitals of the
world. One of the most impressive was unveiled in the
spring of 1965 at historic Runnymede in England. There
it was in 1512 that Magna Carta was born, the great
English document of freedom and liberty that King John
had been forced to sign by his rebellious barons. So it was
a great thing indeed to have the English erect a stone
memorial on this site to an American President and then
have Queen Elizabeth bequeath three acres of its mead-
owland to the American people in his name. Jacqueline
and her children, and other members of the Kennedy
family attended the simple, moving ceremony.

Later Jacqueline issued a statement which said, in
part: "My husband loved history and what you have done
today in his honor would please him more than my words

can express. . . . Your literature and the lives of your great men shaped him, as did no other part of his education. In a sense he returns today to the tradition from which he sprang. . . . For my part I thank you for making it possible for me to be here today with my children. One day they will realize what it means to have their father honored at Runnymede."

No doubt they will. But one day, too, they will look back at those storm-tossed days, swallowed up in the quiet of time, and see another name shining just as brightly next to his, that of their mother. On the clock of history, John F. Kennedy's Presidency—two years, ten months and two days—had been but a moment, brief but unforgettable. A gallant woman had shared that moment with him and left her mark with his. No matter what she did now, or where she went, she would be remembered. Like her husband, Jacqueline Kennedy has a place in history.